KRISHNAMURTI

KRISHNAMURTI
The Reluctant Messiah

by Sidney Field
edited by Peter Hay

PARAGON HOUSE
New York, New York

First edition, 1989
Published in the United States by
Paragon House
90 Fifth Avenue
New York, NY 10011

Editor: Don Fehr
Production Editor: Edward Paige
Copy Editor: John Bergez
Designed by Deirdre C. Amthor

Library of Congress Cataloging-in-Publication Data
Field, Sidney, 1905–1988
    Krishnamurti : the reluctant messiah / by Sidney Field : edited by
Peter Hay.—1st ed.
        p.   cm.
    ISBN 1-55778-180-X
    1. Krishnamurti, J. (Jiddu), 1895–1986.   I. Hay, Peter.
II. Title.
    B5134.K754F54   1989
181'.4—dc20
[B]   89-34009
                                                                        CIP

Manufactured in the United States of America

The paper used in this publication meets the minimum requirements of
American National Standard for Information Sciences—Permanence of
Paper for Printed Materials, ANSI Z39.48-1984.

Because the mind-heart does not know how to sing, it pursues, instead, the singer.

Krishnamurti

Acknowledgments

I AM GRATEFUL FOR THE HELP GIVEN TO ME BY SIDNEY FIELD'S relatives and friends in editing and revising the English-language manuscript of this memoir. My friend Eve Tettemer Siegel was indispensible and unstinting with her personal remembrances and detailed observations which helped to clarify many points in the text. Her sister Joneen Liston, and Sidney's niece, Jeanette Roberts, gave generous access to family photographs and books.

I want to thank Asit Chandmal for his reading of the

manuscript and for his kind permission to quote from his moving diary of Krishnamurti's death. Extracts were published under the title of *The Last Walk,* in "Bombay—The City Magazine" in March 1986; thanks also to William Quinn for sending me a copy. He and others who knew Sidney Field and Krishnamurti well—Daphne Moore Field, Katherine Kiernan and Grayson Rogers—have been most helpful.

I am happy to acknowledge the staff of Paragon House for their professionalism and understanding ways, and especially Don Fehr for editing, and John Bergez for copyediting the manuscript. Finally, I am sure Sidney would join me in giving a large measure of credit to Richard Kahlenberg's tireless efforts in making this English-language edition of his book possible.

Peter Hay

Preface

One has had a vision; one wants to have another; that is all.

W. B. Yeats, on mysticism

FEW AMONG THE GREAT FIGURES OF OUR TIMES ARE AS FASCINAT-
ing and mysterious as Jiddu Krishnamurti, the Indian philosopher, teacher and mystic who died in California in
February 1986, at the age of ninety. He had been in the
public eye almost continuously since his "discovery" at the
age of fourteen in Madras, India, by the Theosophist Soci-

ety, whose European leaders saw him as the future mani-
festation of the Lord Maitreya, the Bodhisattva or Buddha,
the coming World Teacher—or, in Western terms, the Messiah. The little Brahmin boy, of seemingly quite average
talents but of unusual physical beauty, was taken with his
brother, Nitya, to England, where they were given English
clothes and an English education, and taught English manners. Krishnamurti was made president of a new Order of
the Star in the East, which at its height boasted forty-three
thousand members in forty countries. Books and maga-
zines were published in his name; people underwent profound religious experiences in his presence. Then, in 1929,
after his brother's death, and just when his messianic career
was about to be launched, Krishnamurti shocked three
thousand expectant disciples who had gathered on the vast
estate a Dutch aristocrat had given him. He abruptly re-
signed his position as the head of the Order of the Star,
broke with the Theosophist Society, forbade any disciples
to follow him, and set out on a new path of teaching and
urging upon anyone who would listen the need for personal freedom and world peace without nationalism.

Ironically, the Theosophists were proven right when
they recognized in an uneducated Indian boy a genuine
World Teacher, even though he rejected them—and all organized religion—in favor of trying to rid the world of the
need for gurus and messiahs. Courted by the rich and the
powerful, by rationalists and mystics, physicists and artists, Krishnamurti retained to the end a curious mixture of
Eastern thinking and Western manners. He seemed utterly
self-possessed, and at the same time utterly devoid of ego.
He had a dreamy detachment and aloofness, and yet the
ability to communicate with anyone on any level. His personal magnetism was so powerful that it produced unusual

psychic phenomena. He seemed at once utterly serene and totally driven in his fight against the evils of nationalism, possessiveness and muddled thinking. His message, delivered annually in the famous oak groves of Ojai, in his schools in India, England and Switzerland, in dozens of books and tapes, became more and more urgent as he saw the human race approaching the brink of self-annihilation.

The writer Henry Miller, an egotistical sensualist who had a personality as unlike Krishnamurti's as it is possible to have, wrote (*The Books in My Life*, London: Village Press, 1974, P. 153) that "there is no man living whom I would consider it a greater privilege to meet than he." This was his reason: "His career, unique in the history of spiritual leaders, reminds one of the famous Gilgamesh epic. Hailed in his youth as the coming Savior, Krishnamurti renounced the role that was prepared for him, spurned all disciples, rejected all mentors and preceptors. He initiated no new faith or dogma, questioned everything, cultivated doubt (especially in moments of exaltation), and by dint of heroic struggle and perseverance, freed himself of illusion and enchantment, of pride, vanity, and every subtle form of domination over other. . . . Krishnamurti has renounced more than any man I can think of except Christ. . . . He liberated his soul, so to say, from the underworld and the overworld, thus opening to it 'the paradise of heroes.' "

During that long and heroic struggle, Krishnamurti encountered thousands of people, some of whom stayed close to him over many decades. A few wrote books about his life and teachings. Sidney Field, the author of this memoir, knew Krishnamurti for more than sixty years, but did not belong to the inner circle of devotees. They had met when Sidney was still in high school and Krishnamurti, ten years older, was already a world figure. Theirs was a simple and direct friendship, not based on ideological doctrine or affiliation. They shared everyday interests, such as fondness for fast cars and a taste in fine clothes. Gradually, as Sidney matured and began facing the responsibilities of adulthood, he fell under the spell of Krishnamurti's personal magnetism and on occasion sought his guidance. There were times when the older man would not help, and Sidney criticized him to his face in a manner that might have shocked Krishnamurti's more devout followers. But this unique friendship survived precisely because neither of them wanted Sidney to become a disciple.

The subject of this brief book is the course of that friendship. It is not a life of Krishnamurti, nor the autobiography of Sidney Field. The perspective it provides of both men is necessarily fragmentary, glimpses caught in their encounters and correspondence. There are months and years when they did not see each other, and the memoir simply moves on to their next meeting, with little or no connecting material. The author also assumed on the reader's part some knowledge of Krishnamurti's life and of his circle, of Theosophist teaching and history. To make the memoir accessible to a wider readership, the publisher asked Sidney Field to make additions and revisions to the version published in Mexico in 1988, a few weeks before his death. He was already too ill and weak to fulfill this request, and that is how I came to revise and edit the English-language manuscript.

I knew Sidney during the last ten years of his life through my very dear friend Eve Tettemer Siegel, who, being the daughter of Ruth Roberts and John Tettemer, grew up knowing both Krishnamurti and Sidney all her life. It was while visiting Ruth with her that I began to join thousands of ordinary people every spring under the whispering oak trees in Ojai to hear Krishnamurti talk. I had known vaguely of him for some time since Harsh Tanka, one of my Oxford contemporaries, had been teaching at Krishnamurti's School in Brockwod Park, England, and over the years I had read one or two of his books. Still, I went to the Oak Grove the first time with a defiant skepticism, having been inoculated at a young age against ideologies and leaders of any kind. On the West Coast of the North American continent, and in California especially, one is constantly bombarded with lurid news stories of esoteric cults and sinister movements, often associated with Indian gurus. It was startling, then, to hear this seemingly frail and yet ageless man, arguing in a calm, reasoning voice and clipped English accent against gurus, against cults, against any kind of mental or spiritual bondage. I closed my eyes, opened my mind—and I was back in the sunlit Greece of Socrates, and in that timeless landscape of the Buddha under the shady tree; here we were, talking about the same old human problems of how to live together and how to stand alone.

In that quiet, thoughtful crowd there were many who had been listening to this man in that same place for fifty years, including Sidney Field and Ruth Roberts, who had first met in Holland in their early twenties. To my rational mind, this simple fact in itself posed difficult questions. What made thousands of sophisticated people flock every year over half a century to Ojai—and to other places on other continents—to hear the same arguments, presented almost in the same words by a man who did not want any followers? Who was this man, who could be rational and mystical at the same time, who refused to dispense any quick-fix remedies for the chronic ills of the modern world, who claimed no significance for himself, but only for the thoughts and actions he might provoke in his listeners? And how could one *not* think of the phenomenon of the presenter, who had surely one of the most unusual minds of the twentieth century?

Perplexed, I sought out and read the published biographies, which have been written by close associates of Krishnamurti. They are filled with useful facts, but they also leave the subject wrapped in mystery. Perhaps this is a general problem with depicting the great spiritual figures: the more we probe, the more they seem to stand apart from us. Though he encouraged Mary Lutyens to write her books (and urged Sidney Field to publish this memoir), it is difficult to imagine Krishnamurti ever writing an autobiography. He did attempt one when he was twenty, during his messianic period, but the fragment only goes as far as age sixteen. His mature writings reveal no interest in self-analysis. His teaching was almost entirely other-directed, toward the spiritual well-being of the other person; he cared about the impact of the ideas, not whether they were his. In the 1920s, constantly dogged by news reporters, Krishnamurti was often asked how many followers he had. "I do not know how many there are," he would reply in exasperation. "I am not concerned with that. If even one man had been set free, that were enough."

When Sidney first gave me his manuscript to read, I realized that sometimes the best way to see a biographical subject is through the impact he has had on one other person. This is a rare memoir not only because of the unusual portrait it gives of Krishnamurti, but also because of the writer. Its authority comes from a direct and sometimes painful honesty, reflected in its unpretentious style. I have worked hard with Don Fehr, editor at Paragon House, to preserve its charm and personality without overburdening it with more than the necessary historical and background information. Memoirs tend to suggest the past, and Sidney Field gives many unforgettable snapshots of a golden era. But the chief value of his account lies in its detailed and timeless description of the difficulties any ordinary person will encounter on a spiritual quest. Claiming no special expertise or aptitude, he is a guide with whom every reader, young and old, can readily identify. And personally I am grateful to Sidney for taking me to his sunlit valley, speckled with the familiar shadows, rather than leaving me to gaze blindly into the sun.

Peter Hay

Los Angeles. Spring 1989

1

IN MY HOME IN COSTA RICA, WHERE I WAS BORN IN 1905, Krishnamurti was a household word. My parents, grandparents and a few close friends were the original founders of the Theosophical Society in that Central American country. Later, too, they became the first to represent the Order of the Star in the East, founded by Dr. Annie Besant to prepare the way for the coming World Teacher.*

---

* Theosophists believe in the Universal Brotherhood of Man, promote understanding of comparative religion and science, and investigate unexplained laws of

As a small boy, I would often stand gazing at a large, tinted photograph of Krishnamurti, a handsome youth in his Indian clothes, that was prominently displayed in my parents' bedroom, and wonder what kind of a person he really was, whether an ordinary boy like me could some day talk to him and ask his advice. I had heard so much about the great spiritual and social changes he was going to bring about in the world. I wondered if these included limiting parental authority over children, so kids could talk back to them without catching hell, and whether homework would be eliminated.

We were a family of dedicated believers in Krishna-murti and his future role in the world. We believed that it was our good karma to be born at a time when this great man would again reveal to the world the truths that Buddha and Christ had taught. Although we lived in a small, Catholic country, there were no compromises in our stand in this matter. The members of the Order of the Star in the East proudly wore the little five-pointed silver star emblematic of membership in the Order, the men displaying it on the lapel of their coats, the women on their blouses, and ea-

nature, such as psychic phenomena. The Society, based on mystical traditions and teachings that go back thousands of years in India and Western Europe, was founded in America by Madame Helena Petrovna Blavatsky and Colonel Henry Steel Olcott in 1875. Following the death of its founders, Dr. Annie Besant, a charismatic and freethinking Englishwoman, took over the helm of the Society, which in 1882 had moved its headquarters to Adyar, in Madras, India. It was there that Jiddu Khrishnamurti, then an uneducated and inarticulate teenager, was "discovered" by C. W. Leadbeater, one of the leading Theosophists, and later proclaimed as the next incarnation of the Bodhisattva Maitreya, or the Buddha, whom Theosophists also call the World Teacher.

The Theosophical Society prescribed various stages of initiation for the spiritual advancement of the adept. Annie Besant established special sections within the Society, such as the Esoteric Section and the Order of the Star in the East. Sidney Field's parents and their friends became involved in founding and running the Costa Rican chapters of these organizations.

gerly explained its meaning to anyone who inquired. My sister Vera, after marrying into a prominent Catholic family, hung an enlarged photograph of Krishnamurti on the wall in her bedroom, over her side of the double bed. Her husband, Max, the son of a former president of Costa Rica, Bernardo Soto, and a colonel in the nonexistent Costa Rican army, was broad-minded, but also cautious. He promptly hung an equally large photo of the Pope over his side of the bed. An odd pair, those two, presiding over the newlyweds, the old Roman pontiff and the handsome young Brahmin.

We were brought up free of any church influence, but every Sunday morning we attended a sort of Krishnamurti Sunday school, sponsored by the Order of the Star in the East. The proceedings always opened with a declaration of the Order's aims, not unlike a Krishnamurti pledge of allegiance. Stated in florid Spanish, it expressed our belief in the near coming of a great spiritual teacher in the person of Krishnamurti and our commitment to prepare ourselves to be worthy of his teaching. Every youngster in the group took his or her turn reading the pledge. I hated it when my turn came. It was like getting up in class to recite something you hadn't prepared for. In reading it I fumbled, hesitated, coughed, fidgeted. The adult in charge fixed me with a severe look, the other kids giggled, and I felt like a fool. After the pledge came a solemn talk by some prominent Theosophist, exhorting us to live the kind of lives the future World Teacher would approve of. The little ritual became an awful bore, but there was no way out of it. Krishnamurti on Sunday morning was a custom not to be breached.

A custom observed with equal zeal was the wearing of that small, silver star we prized so highly. It was a badge of distinction, and because of violent church opposition to it, it had become synonymous with the cause of individual freedom and civil liberty. The church missed no opportunity to express its feeling on the matter. My brother and I attended a private boys' school where one of the required subjects was Religion, taught by a roly-poly priest. We were excused from class, as were other non-Catholic students, by parental request, but were singled out by the otherwise jovial priest with a stony look as he caught sight of the controversial little star, which we wore in plain sight on our shirts. We wore it in that particular class only, only to taunt the priest, who immediately proceeded to cross himself. We were in league with the devil!

An open fight between the Church Militant and a small but articulate group of intellectuals, artists and *libres pensadores*, or free thinkers, had been threatening for some time and finally broke out over a most unlikely provocation: the issue of new currency put out by the Banco Internacional de Costa Rica, the first nationalized bank in the country, of which my father, Walter J. Field Spencer, became founding president in 1914. To honor him, the bank's board of directors decreed that his picture should appear on the ten-*colón* bills. It did, with the redoubtable little star plainly displayed on his coat lapel. No one would have taken any special notice of it had not the militant clergy raised its loud voice against it in the pages of the government-controlled newspaper, *La Información*. They charged that the heretical Theosophists and members of the infamous Order of the Star in the East had conspired, through the natural flow of currency, to introduce Krishnamurti and his future unholy role into every city, town and village in the country. "The President of the Banco Internacional does not fool us when he wears that little star so blatantly displayed on his coat lapel in his picture on the ten-*colón* bill," they wrote. "For everyone knows that this badge of heresy, which has become the vogue among so many believers, including innocent young people, means only one thing: 'I believe in Krishnamurti!' "

When the church, backed by President Gonzalez Flores' devout wife, launched its major attack on Krishnamurti, the handsome Indian youth seemed destined, in an odd kind of way, to become a factor in the political life of the country. Rising to Krishnamurti's defense was my maternal grandfather, the artist Tomás Povedano de Arcos, whose scathing articles against church bigotry, published in the opposition newspaper, *La Prensa Libre,* rallied the support of a great number of the younger generation. Also coming to the support of Krishnamurti was Federico Tinoco, one of the country's most distinguished and influential citizens. A brilliant man, Oxford-educated, wealthy, member of the Costa Rican Congress, Secretary of War, prominent Theosophist and proud member of the Order of the Star in the East, he was an intimate friend of our family. Keenly aware of political realities and possessed of an insatiable presidential appetite, Tinoco threw himself into the fray. Through public declarations in the press, he taunted President Gonzalez Flores to come out of the safe and unbecoming neutrality he had assumed in the Krishnamurti affair. Counting on his large popular support, Tinoco sharply denounced his superior for hiding behind his wife's Catholic skirts instead of coming to the defense of the civil liberties he had pledged to support. Government supporters demanded Tinoco's resignation, but the president kept him on, presumably figuring he could keep a more effective handle on his maverick cabinet officer while he had him in government harness than out of it.

The church versus Krishnamurti was the hottest issue

of the day. It culminated in the burning of the beautiful and newly built Theosophical Temple, where members of the Order of the Star met. A wild-eyed priest proudly confessed to setting the place on fire. There were loud public protests, mostly among students, against the government and the church. The bitter conflict played right into Tinoco's clever hands. In 1917 he overthrew the conservative, church-backed government of Gonzalez Flores in a daring coup d'état.

The new president had great plans for the country, and the country looked to him with great expectations. A staunch supporter of Krishnamurti, he saw to it that translated excerpts of Krishnamurti's little book, *At the Feet of the Master*, appeared regularly in *La Información*.

It was a time for celebration. Parties and banquets honored the new, progressive president. Lotus Day, the anniversary of Buddha's birth, celebrated by Buddhists the world over on the eighth of May, was a day of special meaning to Theosophists and members of the Order of the Star in the East. Each year my family, as the leading Theosophists in the country, observed the occasion by hosting a big reception. This particular one was a black-tie affair in honor of President Tinoco. Important public figures attended. Some cabinet officers, wishing to please the chief executive, had joined the Theosophical Society and the Order of the Star in the East. Indeed, membership in these two organizations had become fashionable. Some considered it daring, a way of telling the church they were emancipated. Politicians who courted the president's favor pretended to embrace Theosophy and the belief in Krishnamurti's future role, then went to church on Sunday to confess their sin.

All of them gathered this evening in the large and

elegant living room of our townhouse in San José, Costa Rica's capital, and mingled with the faithful. It was a lively and noisy crowd. At one end of the room, near the Steinway Grand, stood two large easels holding portraits of Mme. Blavatsky and Krishnamurti, painted by my grandfather, Tomás Povedano de Arcos, former *pintor de cámara*, or court painter, to Queen Cristina of Spain. His painting of the Russian founder of the Theosophical Society was rather forbidding; it showed her with an intense, glum and melancholy look and a drab shawl around her head. But the painting of Krishnamurti, with the sky-blue turban and golden dhoti, was beautiful, I always thought. The two paintings, standing side by side on their easels, exhibited an extraordinary contrast in attitude and color.

The president's wife, Maria de Tinoco, a close friend of my mother's, opened the proceedings. She was a very nice lady, tall and corpulent, with a pretty, girlish face and a soft, caressing voice. She was also very emotional, and when she spoke about Krishnamurti her voice became tremulous and her large bosom heaved. High-sounding oratory by others followed, extolling the great mission of Mme. Blavatsky and the even more important promise of the mission of Krishnamurti. Then there were musical offerings—piano, violin, voice. My sister Flora generally sang on these occasions. Champagne and refreshments completed the festivities. There were laughter and good fellowship, and even a few happily unsteady celebrants among those who proudly wore their bright little silver stars.

The following morning Mme. Blavatsky's portrait was hauled off to the Theosophical Lodge, while Krishnamurti's portrait went back to my grandfather's studio. I felt sad to see it go. It seemed to belong in our living room, but my grandfather was very possessive about it. In our family Krishnamurti had become like a distant relative in a faraway land who had attained notoriety and fame—a celebrity whom one hopefully wished to meet some day.

Exactly twenty days later we celebrated another anniversary: my birthday. Doña Maria, the first lady of Costa Rica, aware that we were planning eventually to move to the United States, gave me a little book she thought would improve my English, and my character. It was *At the Feet of the Master*, a summary of meditations Krishnamurti published in English as his first book, when he was only fifteen. The book accomplished neither of Doña Maria's objectives; indeed, it distressed my father to hear me read from it. He determined that something must be done at once to improve my English. I had dire thoughts of being interned in the English School in San José. Mercifully, Doña Maria came up with a happy solution. Her older sister, Marian Le Capellain, a stern spinster who lived with the Tinocos, had been educated in England. She had agreed, we were told, to teach my brother and me properly to speak the King's English.

It was fun being driven every morning to the presidential mansion, past the military guard at the gate, armed with my copy of *At the Feet of the Master*. Miss LeCapellain, who didn't share her sister's or brother-in-law's philosophical views, and who was obviously less than ecstatic about her new educational chore, met the challenge with another book, the Bible, which she read to us daily. But her habit of being late for class in the book-lined library, and mine of curiously snooping around the presidential domicile while my brother entertained himself with a Spanish version of "The Katzenjammer Kids," published in a local newspaper, produced an unexpected and delightful bonus: a close and cozy friendship with the president, whom I first discovered alone in the formal dining room having his breakfast. He was no stranger to me, nor I to him. I had known him, through my family, as long as I could remember, but on a rather formal, distant basis. Here we chatted informally as he offered me *pan dulce* and cookies while he sipped his black coffee and munched on a piece of toast with marmalade. We talked about his exploits as a former soccer star, and his horsemanship. He loved horses. He told me stories of derring-do, corrected my pronunciation when I read to him from *At the Feet of the Master*, hoping to get his very British sister-in-law off my back, and told jokes. We laughed, and sometimes we even gossiped. I was always fascinated by the man, by his extraordinary looks and his apparently endless collection of resplendent uniforms. He always seemed enormously self-confident, but sometimes, glimpsing him in repose, I had a feeling that there was a great sadness behind his eyes.

Tinoco was a commanding figure, tall and powerfully built. In his youth he had reportedly been very handsome, but somewhere along his youthful path he had contracted a venereal disease that robbed him of every strand of hair on his body. In Paris he had achieved a partial restoration of his former looks by means of a rakish toupee, painted black eyebrows and long, artificial eyelashes. Because his skin had assumed an unhealthy whiteness, his large black eyes appeared blacker than a crow's plumage, and because life had embittered him, they shone with an angry light— except when he visited at breakfast with the young boy who had trouble with his English and looked up to him in awe. Then he was always gentle, kind and patient. "Don Pelico," as he was affectionately known among his friends, was a remarkable man, a character right out of the Middle Ages.

The country basked in an era of reason, open friendship and optimism.

Krishnamurti's stock rose dramatically.

Unfortunately, Tinoco's regime lasted only two years. His ship of state ran into rough seas when Washington refused to recognize his administration because he had come to power through force. None of the loans he was depending on came through, with the result that his most important projects went down the drain. Nevertheless, Tinoco was determined to succeed and tried to get loans from European governments. He told my father, who had unsuccessfully interceded in his behalf in Washington, that before he was through he would create in Costa Rica a society Krishnamurti would be proud of. But as opposition to his government hardened in Washington, and leading European governments turned a cold shoulder, Tinoco, the man of ideals and principle, gradually turned into the man of power, blindly self-seeking. Frustrated and bedeviled at every turn, he dissolved the Legislative Assembly and became the first dictator in Costa Rica's history.

During 1919 Tinoco's troubles mounted daily. Another close friend of our family, Julio Acosta, a noted educator, prominent Theosophist and member of the Order of the Star in the East, gathered an army of volunteers in the province of Guanacaste and started an advance against the dictator in San José. Tinoco's brother, Joaquin, to whom he was devoted, was assassinated. Meanwhile the U.S. cruiser *Lexington* dropped anchor in Costa Rica's Caribbean Bay of Limón, ready for any emergency. An unruly crowd of pro-Tinoco young people stoned the American Legation in San José and tried to set it on fire, an event which, on top of other problems, sent the harassed minister, Benjamin Chase, a friend of ours, back to the States with a nervous breakdown.

Tinoco saw the handwriting on the wall and decided to act quickly. He stormed into the Banco Internacional and angrily demanded from my father that he turn over to him all the bank's cash reserves—$35 million, a trifle in these inflationary days, but in the mid-1920s and in little Costa Rica, a considerable sum. Walter Field refused. The dictator, crazed with grief over his brother's death and his imminent separation from his family, friends and country, turned against my father. He accused him of having had a hand in the latest Washington maneuvers and of joining forces with Acosta behind his back. He claimed that he had spent his personal fortune fighting rebellious groups all over the country and charged "the bandit Acosta" with stealing his valuable properties in Guanacaste. Somebody had to pay for all that!

My father's response was to hand in his resignation, together with those of the entire board of directors. The press got wind of the sensational story and spread the news. It was an overnight national scandal, and the end of Tinoco. But he hung on long enough to grab the bank's cash reserves before fleeing to France.

The church, emboldened by the turn of events, returned to its attack on Krishnamurti. How could a supporter of Krishnamurti such as Tinoco do differently?

The days that followed were chaotic. Acosta's troops had not yet reached the capital, and the country was without a government. Roving bands sacked stores and fought openly in the streets. Citizens fortified their homes against marauders. Our own home was under machine-gun fire for three days while we huddled in the cavernous wine cellar. Tinoco later disclaimed all responsibility for this wanton attack. We believed him; perhaps we had to, considering our long and close friendship. It was true that my father had political enemies in the country, that Tinoco was not in command at the time and that it was open season, a time to settle old feuds. At any rate, life was hard and unpredictable during those dying days of the Tinoco regime.

Krishnamurti's stock plummeted.

Eventually, Julio Acosta, the new hero, and his ragtag army of volunteers entered a nearly deserted San José, and none too soon: living in a dank wine cellar was not our idea of home, sweet home. Inaugurated president in 1920, Acosta promptly reinstated the publication of translated excerpts from *At the Feet of the Master* in *La Información*. He offered amnesty to his former enemies and, like Tinoco, celebrated a new era of freedom and respect for minorities. Life returned to normalcy.

Krishnamurti's stock began a slow recovery.

2

A few years later, in the summer of 1925, we had just settled in our new home in Hollywood and were awaiting Krishnamurti and his brother, Nitya, who had been invited over for tea. My father had already met Krishnamurti, for he had made a trip to Los Angeles alone before deciding to sell our coffee plantation in Costa Rica and settle in Hollywood.

I was in my late teens, and for me the impending visit was a momentous occasion. After all my years of hearing about Krishnamurti and his mission, contemplating his picture and thinking about him, he was finally going to come to life. I was thrilled, but also disturbed. I was sure he would see right through me—just an ordinary boy who had completely failed to live up to the precepts of the Order of the Star. I wished the visit could be postponed. If I tried hard, I might be able to improve myself, but I needed time. It was the middle of the week when my father announced that the visit would take place that Sunday—not much time for self-improvement! I was greatly tempted to feign illness, or to stay away on the pretext of having to attend an extra-curricular school activity. But the desire to meet the World Teacher overrode all other considerations. I waited for their arrival upstairs, looking out a window into the street, my heart beating fast.

At long last a sleek black limousine stopped in front of the house. Two slim, smartly dressed young men stepped out of it. I immediately recognized Krishnamurti. He and his brother walked slowly toward the front door, stopping for a second to check the house number over the front porch. When the doorbell rang, my heart was pounding so wildly against my ribs I thought it must be heard by every-one. I heard my father's voice greeting them in the entrance hall, and their answering voices. My mother, my sister Flora and my brother, John, were then introduced, and they all went into the living room. My mother called to me. There was no escape now. My knees felt weak, and my mouth tasted like sawdust.

Father introduced me to the visitors, who smiled, called me by my first name and shook hands. Each of them said something which I didn't really hear for the thumping of my heart. Krishnamurti's wonderfully expressive black eyes were fully on me as I stood staring at him, speechless

14

and immobile. I think he was conscious of my overly excited inner state, for he took his attention off me momentarily and talked to other members of the family. I was grateful to him for that. Soon I began to regain my composure.

Nitya, well informed on the world situation, took command of the conversation. Annie Besant had taken the two boys to England while they were still in their teens for a proper education, which took better with Nitya than with his older brother. He spoke with the polish of an English gentleman, and with incisive wit tore into the inflated postures of various world leaders in the news. Nitya was very funny and had us all in stitches, particularly his brother, who would explode with his contagious, boyish laughter. A well-known newspaper writer friend of ours, who had begged to be introduced to Krishnamurti, was the only other person present besides the family at that little tea party. Afterward, he remarked that although Krishnamurti was much the better looking of the two, in his opinion Nitya was cast more in the mold of future World Teacher. Everyone was very much impressed with Nitya. He had a special charm, and he made you feel at ease with him. But Krishnamurti's physical beauty and the extraordinary and luminous quality of purity that radiated from him set him apart. The usually cynical Bernard Shaw, after meeting Krishnamurti, described him as "the most beautiful human being he ever saw." Whether you believed in the claims made for him or not, everyone who met him agreed that he was indeed special and unique, all the more so because he seemed totally unaware of the fact that he was not like other men.

He was so unassuming and vibrantly alive that you were immediately drawn to him. He asked about Costa Rica and said he would like to visit it some day. Then, turning to me, he inquired about my activities at Hollywood High School. I had to admit I was not a particularly good student, but, I added, I managed to get by. He laughed and said that he, too, had been a poor student. He was leaving shortly for Europe, he told me, then India, before returning to Ojai, a little town about eighty-five miles north of Los Angeles. He asked me to visit him there, which pleased me immensely.

Before leaving Krishnamurti brought up a subject that instantly touched a response in all of us. He spoke about Federico Tinoco, who by this time had become a legend in Monte Carlo, where he had lost part of his ill-gotten fortune on the gaming tables. He told us that he had met the ex-dictator recently in Paris, and that he and his wife had invited him to dinner. They had been charming to him and had spoken with concern and affection about the Field family. Then Krishnamurti told us a story that was entirely typical of him. After dinner, he related, Tinoco took a small box out of his pocket, opened it to reveal a dazzling collection of diamonds of various shapes and sizes, and offered him his pick. Krishnamurti politely refused the generous gift, saying they were all beautiful but that he was not interested in diamonds. I thought, my God, it takes a lot of character to refuse such a gift. When my father told him about the great support Tinoco had given Krishnamurti in Costa Rica, he was surprised, for the ex-dictator had not mentioned it, even though his wife had said that they had been staunch supporters since the founding of the Order of the Star in the East. To our repeated inquiries about our former great friends in Costa Rica, Krishnamurti's responses were purposely vague, or perhaps he just didn't know the answers. He did, however, very clearly remember the man's extraordinary appearance. Tinoco had discarded his flamboyant uniforms and chose to appear in public draped in a long, black cape with red lining and wearing a jaunty *sombrero cordobés*, the traditional Andalusian hat, on his head.

I think Nitya, who was suffering from tuberculosis, was not feeling well at this point, because Krishnamurti kept glancing at him with concern. Suddenly he got up to go. I had heard my father refer to the young Indian teacher as Krishnaji, but I didn't know whether it would be proper for me to address him likewise, so as we were walking out to the car after the visit I asked him, "Should I call you Mr. Krishnamurti, or Mr. Krishnaji?"

He smiled, amused, and said simply, "Call me Krishna."

Some months after that first meeting, Nitya died in Ojai while his brother was on his journey to India. Krishnamurti has written about the great grief he suffered when he heard of his brother's death, and of the mystical union he had felt: "On the physical plane we could be separated and now we are inseparable . . . For my brother and I are one. As Krishnamurti I now have greater zeal, greater faith, greater sympathy and greater love, for there is also in me the body, the Being, of Nityananda." It was a turning point in his life.

Upon his return to the States, I called him in Ojai. We made an appointment to meet at the home of Mr. and Mrs. John Ingleman, where he always stayed while in Hollywood. I was still very self-conscious and shy with him, and since he has never been known as a great extrovert, our conversation was necessarily somewhat labored. There was, however, one subject that mutually interested us and helped establish an easy rapport: automobiles. I found out that he knew a great deal about them and that he loved fast and expensive European cars. He had a big Lincoln, he told me, but was going to trade it in for a Packard, which in his opinion was the best American car. He promised to let me drive it. He was curious about the kind of car I was driving and accompanied me outside to see it. It was neither a Packard nor a Lincoln, but for a kid of eighteen it was a car to be proud of, an elegant-looking Jordan, long since gone. It had been custom-built for the celebrated Metropolitan diva Geraldine Farrar, and my father had bought it in Hollywood for my brother and me for a fraction of its original cost.

Some weeks later I visited Krishnamurti at Arya Vihara, the six-acre estate which Mrs. Besant bought for him in the Ojai Valley, whose name in Sanskrit meant "the monastery of the noble ones." He had already acquired his Packard and reveled in showing me all its special features. It was beautiful, a sky-blue, sleek, convertible roadster. He did not ask me to try it out, and I was relieved. The idea of putting a scratch on this beauty froze me with apprehension. He told me proudly the time he had made with it on his first trip from Hollywood to Ojai. I was envious. He asked what my best time was. I hated to admit it, but it was much slower than his. I vowed to myself I must do something about it. I stayed for lunch and met Rama Rao, one of Krishnamurti's close associates, a sweet and gentle person with soft, doe-like eyes twinkling with humor.

A couple of weeks later I paid another visit to Arya Vihara. This time I drove the family Cadillac. (My father would never lend me his new Cadillac for any other reason than to go and see Krishnaji in Ojai.) I had managed to cut his time by two minutes and a half! He was surprised but a little skeptical. I was prepared for that, however: I showed him a stopwatch I had set upon leaving my home in Hollywood, and the time it marked as I arrived at Arya Vihara. He was convinced, but instead of congratulations he gave me a little lecture about speeding which somehow lacked conviction. I promised him I'd take it easy. After all, there was no reason to speed now: the new record had been set.

We went inside, and I met Rajagopal for the first time.* I liked him. He had a good, quick mind and a sense of humor. We had lunch, and then Krishnaji took his siesta. Later we went out for a long walk behind Arya Vihara and had our first serious talk. I asked him whether he was in contact with Nitya on the other side. "Nitya is here," he said. "He sends his love." But he would not elaborate. When I pressed him for an explanation, he stopped dead in his tracks and looked straight at me. He said the important thing was not whether the personality survives bodily death but the quality of relationship here and now.

"Have you always been clairvoyant?" I asked him, hoping to draw him out on that subject.

"Clairvoyance doesn't really help," he said. "I can see my family in India any time I want to. They're all starving."

When we got back to the house, Topa Topa, the highest peak of that broken range of mountains that cradles the valley, was bathed for a brief period in a soft, rose-purple hue that is not to be found on any painter's palette.

---

* As a thirteen-year-old boy, D. Rajagopalacharya had been another "discovery" of C. W. Leadbeater, and at first was perceived as a rival to the claim that Krishnamurti would be the next World Teacher. Later they became close associates, and after his brother Nitya's death, Krishnamurti appointed Rajagopal secretary of the Order of the Star. After managing Krishnamurti's business affairs for thirty-five years, Rajagopal broke their connection in 1960, while attempting to retain control over Krishnamurti Writings, Inc. (KWInc.), the foundation that owned all of K's copyrights, as well as his schools and other real estate.

The estrangement led to a break between K's friends and associates, and to a number of lawsuits, the last of which was not finally settled until the summer of 1986, just after K's death.

I returned to Arya Vihara a couple of weeks later. Krishnaji appeared to be in great shape. Sometimes he seemed a bit tired and haggard; on this day he was radiant. He was outside doing some gardening and came directly to my car before I had a chance to get out. Gleefully, he related that a few days before he had driven to Hollywood in the Packard and had broken my record by a full two minutes! Before I could say anything, he exclaimed, "Smoke that!"

"Didn't you get a speeding ticket?" I asked, hoping that he had.

He laughed and shook his head, like a kid who had done something naughty and gotten away with it. It had been early in the morning, he said, and there had been hardly any traffic on the road. Still, it was an impressive performance. I knew how fast I had driven to set the previous record, and what chances I had taken.

"I can't compete with you. You have the Masters on your side."

Krishnaji laughed and pointed at his Packard in the garage. "That's on my side," he said. Thus ended my racing competition with Krishnaji. A sleek Packard roadster and what I considered the protection of the White Brotherhood* were odds I couldn't beat.

Krishnaji was very much interested in what young people were thinking and feeling, and he asked me if he could meet some of my young friends. That was easy. With the extensive media exposure he was getting, everyone wanted to meet him, especially girls, who considered him "dreamy." The girl I was going with at the time, Dorothy

---

* According to Mme. Blavatsky, all the Initiates form and belong to one of the three lodges of the Great White Brotherhood, located in Luxor, Egypt, in the Himalayas and in Greece.

Taft, a pretty young lady whose father, a prominent realtor, had developed and subdivided most of West Hollywood, was delighted at the prospect of meeting the handsome young Brahmin. She collected a group of her friends who were attending the exclusive Marlborough School for Girls, some eighteen or twenty of them, all very attractive and impressionable. We met at her home on Sunset Boulevard on a warm Sunday afternoon.

Krishnaji was very nervous and wondered what he should talk about to a crowd of young girls. I told him not to worry, that the girls were probably not so much interested in what he had to say as in looking at him and being with him in the same room. That made him all the more nervous.

Dorothy's parents and her actress sister, Sally, met us at the front door. Then Dorothy escorted Krishnaji, elegantly attired, into the living room. I was behind him and could hear the subdued "aahs" and "ohhs" of the excited girls as he came into view. Dorothy introduced him much as you would a motion picture superstar. He glanced apprehensively at me and sat down, surrounded by a semicircle of lovely teenage girls, all of them eager to be impressed. Seated on chairs and cushions on the floor, they kept their eyes riveted on the handsome but uncomfortably self-conscious young man from India. He fumbled with his handkerchief and wiped perspiration from his face. So did I. The silence that ensued began to worry me. What if he just sits there in utter silence, I thought. I had had experience of how easily Krishnaji could lapse into a long, deep silence. Then a sudden change occurred in him. Calm and composed, he began to speak. He spoke about the different lifestyles of American and Indian young people, their different attitudes toward courtship, marriage and the raising

21

of a family. The girls seemed to love the short talk. There were questions afterward, which he answered very adequately, I thought. Some of the girls had bought copies of *At the Feet of the Master* and rushed to him for his autograph. There were some refreshments and many thanks, after which the girls insisted that he come to their school and speak to the entire student body. Krishnaji promised he would, and we left.

Getting into the car, he asked me if I thought he had handled the situation well. I told him he had handled it beautifully. For the first time I reflected on the interesting phenomenon that would occur many times in the future, when the shy, uncertain and self-conscious young man would suddenly become full of poise and authority.

Driving him back to the Inglemans', I asked whether he had been aware of the strong atmosphere of sex pervading the living room.

"Of course," he replied.

"Isn't it distracting?" I asked. "What can you do about it?"

"You bank your sex force. You don't let it disturb you."

"You're different," I said. "It's very hard to control thoughts. They go where they want to. I'm sure every girl in that room was fantasizing about getting in bed with you."

"Oh, my God!" he exclaimed.

That weekend Krishnaji's Packard either was being serviced or loaned to a friend. At any rate, he was to be without a car, and I volunteered to drive for him. He made me feel I was doing him a great favor when in fact it was the other way around. He asked whether I could pick him up at the Ambassador Hotel the following day before dinner, around six. He gave me the room number I should go to, and left it at that.

Promptly at six I drove into the Ambassador Hotel

parking lot and went directly to the room he had indicated, full of curiosity about who he was meeting there. My imagination was running to all kinds of things.

I knocked at the door and waited. Then I heard somebody's steps approaching. The door opened, and I was face to face with John Barrymore. The great actor looked me up and down rather disdainfully. I said I was there to pick up Mr. Krishnamurti. Recognizing my voice, Krishnaji came over and introduced me. Barrymore gave me a gruff "How do you do" and turned around and went back inside, probably wondering why Krishnamurti allowed his chauffeur to appear on duty without his uniform.

As I drove him home, Krishnaji told me that he had met Barrymore through the actor's agent, Henry Hotchener, whom I knew, and who was married to the former opera singer Marie Russak, a prominent Theosophist friend of Annie Besant.

Krishnaji liked Barrymore. He thought he was an interesting, witty man. I asked him, "What do you talk about with Barrymore?"

"The Buddha's life, mostly," he answered. He explained that Barrymore was interested in Buddhism and thought that the Buddha's renunciation was one of the most dramatic and inspiring events in history. The actor had told him that he would love to play the role of Buddha in a movie but so far hadn't been able to sell the idea to any of the movie moguls.

Krishnaji, who always emphasized the positive side of a person's character, was impressed by the fact that Barrymore, an alcoholic, totally abstained from liquor on those particular weekends when he came with John Jr., his young son, to visit him. To Krishnaji that was a sacrifice born of love that commanded respect.

Krishnaji had invited the celebrated actor to come to

Arya Vihara in Ojai and have lunch with him. Barrymore delightedly accepted the invitation, after solemnly promising to keep the appointed day the soberest of his life.

Free from any alcoholic influences, John Barrymore set out for Ojai on a bright and sunny morning to spend the day with his distinguished friend. While driving through the town of Ventura, however, he was seized with thirst. He parked his custom-built Lincoln convertible outside a bar and went in to ask for a glass of water. According to his account, the waiter brought him a beer instead. You can never rely on waiters, he later told Krishnaji, tongue in cheek. Contemplating the cool, frothy, golden liquid, he thought: what's one little beer to a man of purpose? Another little beer followed, then another, and then another. How many, he couldn't recall. Some time later, his thirst quenched, he got into his car and resumed his journey. Miraculously, he arrived at Arya Vihara in one piece, though he was more than an hour late for lunch. Krishnaji, the perfect host, had waited for him. Barrymore staggered out of his car. With an unsteady gait he managed to climb the porch steps of Arya Vihara, knocked at the door—and practically fell into Krishnaji's arms.

Krishnaji, who was highly amused at the incident, told me that Barrymore, despite his state of intoxication, was a perfect gentleman throughout the visit, telling funny stories at the luncheon table, poking fun at some of the top stars in Hollywood and drinking gallons of black coffee.

Afraid that the noted visitor might not be able to make it back to Hollywood, Krishnaji invited him to stay overnight. Barrymore wouldn't hear of it; he could never put Krishnaji to such an inconvenience. He had made it to Ojai, and he would damn well make it back to Hollywood. And so he did.

The next day, realizing that things had not gone according to form, Barrymore wrote Krishnaji a letter apologizing for his fall from grace. He enclosed a large photograph of himself, dedicated "to the only man I have ever met who treads the path of the great Indian Prince, Siddartha Gautama." In his letter, Barrymore added that he was more determined than ever to do the life of Buddha on film, with a slight change in the casting: Krishnaji would play Buddha, with Barrymore cast as Buddha's favorite disciple, Ananda. Obviously, he was now thinking of The Life of Ananda, with Buddha in a supporting role!*

The following week Krishnaji was back in Hollywood to visit with us. He had promised to come to dinner, as he often did in those days. He enjoyed coming to our home; he liked my mother's vegetarian cooking, especially her Spanish rice, my brother John's stories about his latest amorous adventures, and simply being treated as a normal human being in a family that loved him.

I remember this occasion particularly well because it had been a most trying day for my father, who was president of the Field Building & Loan Association. That afternoon he had fired his secretary-treasurer, a man by the name of Charles Matthei, after a stormy session. Matthei, who had a vile temper, had sworn to kill my father before the day was

* The idea of Krishnamurti acting in a film was not as far-fetched as people might think who knew him only in the second half of his life. Following his arrival in New York City in August 1926 (the year that the Order of the Star in the East had reached a membership of forty-three thousand members in forty countries), the exotic and improbably handsome Krishnamurti became a national celebrity, pursued by the media wherever he went. In some ways his celebrity status was that of a movie star, except that it endured longer and the Hollywood community paid him deference rarely granted to an actor. Anita Loos, in her autobiographical book, Kiss Hollywood Good-by, gives a delightful vignette of a picnic in the dry Los Angeles riverbed, which included Charlie Chaplin, Paulette Goddard, Greta Garbo, Aldous Huxley and Christopher Isherwood, as well as K and Miss Loos.

over. Anxiously we awaited Krishnaji's arrival. We felt that so long as he was in the house, nothing violent could happen.

Krishnaji was always promptly on time. This evening, as if he knew the situation, he arrived early, much to our relief. As he entered and greeted the family, I noticed that he kept his right hand extended slightly in front of him, rather stiffly. He asked me where the bathroom was, and after showing him, I inquired whether he had injured his hand. "No," he replied. "It's Norma Talmadge's perfume." He explained that earlier in the evening Barrymore had taken him to Norma Talmadge's home and that he couldn't get rid of her perfume after she shook his hand.

At the dinner table my father told Krishnaji about the Matthei incident and the man's angry threat. As we finished eating, Mother remarked how thankful she was that nothing untoward had happened, doubtless as a result of Krishnaji's beneficent presence, a remark which embarrassed him. A moment later there was a loud knock at the front door. The sound had an amazing physical effect on us all, as if we had suddenly been connected to a live electrical wire. We were literally lifted off our chairs, especially Krishnaji. All of us had the same thought: Matthei is out there with a gun!

We stared at one another, speechless. The suspense was unbearable. I glanced over at Krishnaji. His serene expression reassured me. Quickly I got up and went to the door.

The caller was a carpet salesman! Loudly, so the others would know we were safe, I told him we were not buying carpets tonight. I could hear them laughing with relief as the dispirited salesman shuffled off disappointedly under his load of carpets.

With the subject of facing danger on all our minds, Krishnaji told us of an occasion when he was walking alone in Yosemite National Park and a huge grizzly bear came menacingly toward him. Krishnaji stood silently before the animal, only a few feet away from him, quite calm and unafraid, so he said. They eyed each other for a long moment, and then the bear quietly ambled off. So did Krishnaji. But when he got back to the safety of the inn where he was staying, his body trembled all over. He explained that fear is often a purely physical reaction of the body when it senses danger to itself.

3

I SAW KRISHNAJI SEVERAL TIMES BEFORE HE DEPARTED FOR EUrope and India that year. On one occasion we went to the movies together—the cinema, as he called it—and dined together. He asked me what young people my age were doing and thinking. I said they were mostly interested in sports, sex and rebelling against authority.

"To rebel without intelligence leads nowhere," he said, a remark he had expressed before.

"Why don't you tell them that yourself," I suggested. "It

would be wonderful if you could speak in assembly at Hollywood High School. The kids would love to hear you."

Krishnaji agreed that this was a good idea: he would like to do it. Unfortunately, it was never done. Soon after our conversation he left the country, and upon his return the following year I had already graduated from Hollywood High. Nevertheless, I pursued the matter, but a suitable date could not be immediately arranged, and the whole thing eventually disappeared down that well-known road of good intentions.

Knowing that I led an active social life, Krishnaji asked me if, before leaving, I could take him to one of the parties I went to. He was interested in observing young people close at hand. I said I would be very happy to do so. But no sooner had I said it than I could have bitten my tongue off for having agreed so readily. There was no question that the parties I attended in those school days were not exactly the kind to bring Krishnamurti to. There were other kinds of parties among Hollywood school kids, of course, "nice" parties, as adults liked to call them, properly chaperoned, but I generally managed to avoid them, with the result that I was seldom invited to them. So the prospect of introducing Krishnaji to Hollywood's younger generation at play be-came dimmer every day that passed. I hated to disappoint him, but there seemed no solution to the problem. Then, out of the blue, a friend I hadn't seen for some time called to invite me to a party at his home. I immediately accepted, and asked if I could bring Krishnaji along. He was startled by my request and thought I was putting him on. When I explained the situation he said, of course, he would be greatly honored. The boy who was giving the party was Stanley Rogers, whose younger brother, Grayson, a fine professional athlete, was a good friend of mine, and whose father, L. W. Rogers, was then president of the American Section of the Theosophical Society. Stanley belonged to a newly organized group called The Young Theosophists of America, of which I, for a brief period, had served as president after inexplicably being elected to that office.

I drove to Arya Vihara to give Krishnaji the cheerful news. He asked me, with proper concern, what kind of a party it would be, for I had previously described—with tact and restraint, of course—some of the parties I had attended. "This is really a nice party," I assured him, feigning enthusiasm. "And we can leave any time you want to." I didn't dare to tell him it was a young Theosophists' party, because I thought he might throw up his hands in dismay. He did not enjoy the solemnity of such events, and he clearly wanted to "observe" young people, and not those who already looked upon him as a guru or messiah.

When we arrived at the Rogers home on Argyle Avenue in Hollywood, we stood at the open door for a moment, watching the young couples dance. It was the "in" thing in those days to dance as close together as you could manage. After a moment's contemplation of the scene, Krishnaji gave me a perplexed look. Just then the host recognized us and came over to greet us. The music stopped. Then Mrs. Rogers, a charming and gracious lady, took Krishnaji by the hand and introduced him to the surprised young crowd. The girls were thrilled, and immediately surrounded the handsome Brahmin. The music started again. Would he dance? they asked. Would he talk to them later? Would he have some cake and punch? Shyly, Krishnaji kept backing away from the insistent bevy, right up to the living room wall behind him. Cornered, he was looking anxiously for a way out when a big, bosomy lass reached out to him, took hold of his arm and invited him to dance. Krishnaji pro-

31

tested that he didn't know how. She brushed aside his objection: she'd teach him. With that, the girl put her arm firmly around him and literally dragged him onto the dance floor, all the while swinging her hips in rhythm with the music. The other dancers, sensing something unusual was about to happen, discreetly withdrew to the sidelines in expectation of watching the World Teacher do the foxtrot. The buxom girl kept urging him on, but Krishnaji wouldn't budge. He turned and looked appealingly at me. Ready to dance myself, there was nothing I could do, or wanted to do. All at once, he pried himself loose from the dancer's embrace, turned and walked determinedly towards me. "Sidney, take me home," he said bluntly. With Krishnaji apologizing for his abrupt departure, we left the party.

"My God, the way they dance!" he exclaimed in the car.

"That's the way all young people dance."

"It's a form of sex," he said sententiously.

If it had been anyone else I would have argued the point, but Krishnaji was not like anyone else. It was perfectly clear that dancing was not his strong suit. So be it.

The following year Krishnaji returned to Ojai with Dr. Besant, Rajagopal and Rosalind Williams.* The devout had arranged a welcome for him and Dr. Besant at the Southern Pacific station in downtown Los Angeles. Besides a small crowd of curious spectators, there must have been some three hundred or so devotees, mostly women, excitedly holding bouquets of flowers in their hands. My father,

---

* Rosalind Williams, a close associate of Krishnamurti, nursed Nitya through his final illness. She married Rajagopal in 1927.

brother and I were also among those present to welcome him, sans flowers.

As Krishnaji and Dr. Besant walked along the concourse toward John Ingleman's waiting limousine, there was a chorus of welcoming shouts from the women, who started to throw flowers at their feet. Krishnaji recognized us just then, waved a hand and proceeded to do a nimble danse macabre trying to sidestep the tender things at his feet. One of the curious bystanders next to my father turned to him and said, "If that's the Christ, I'm the Devil's brother!" My father fixed him with a stern look and said, "Maybe you are."

Battling through the shower of flowers, Krishnaji and Dr. Besant finally made it to the waiting car. I caught a glimpse of Krishnaji sitting next to the window, a forlorn and puzzled expression on his face as the flowers kept coming his way, smashing against the window pane and collecting on the car top and hood. By the time they pulled away, the Ingleman limousine, laden with welcoming flowers, looked like a funeral hearse.

A few days later Krishnaji called to invite me to Dr. Besant's lecture at the Philharmonic Auditorium in Los Angeles. Since Krishnaji and Rajagopal were driving in from Ojai, I met them at a box they had reserved close to the stage. The place was packed. Punctually at eight-thirty, Dr. Besant stepped onto the huge stage of the Philharmonic, dressed in a long-sleeved, flowing gown that matched the silvery white of her wavy hair. As she acknowledged the audience's applause, I kept thinking how very small she looked on that huge stage, and how paralyzed with stage fright I would be in her place. Dr. Besant, Krishnaji had told me, was one of the greatest orators in the world, but I wondered whether she would be able to hold this restless audience. She stood silent and erect before the lectern, waiting for the crowd to quiet down. Then she started to speak, slowly and deliberately, with that beautiful, distinctive diction of the cultivated Britisher, and a magnificent command of the language. As she got into her subject, "Civilization, Its Past and Future," Mrs. Besant unleashed a power that kept the audience riveted to their seats. An extraordinary transformation had taken place. The little white-haired lady who stepped onto the lecture platform became a commanding force of tremendous stature, holding the capacity audience in the hollow of her hand. She spoke without notes, and without the slightest hesitation— always the right word, the right intonation, the right climax at the right moment. It was a masterly exhibition of oratory and an amazing display of historical knowledge. Krishnaji had asked me to go to Ojai toward the end of the week and meet Dr. Besant personally, so I left right after the lecture, glad to avoid the crush of people that were attempting to go backstage to meet the famous Theosophist.

Some days later I shook hands with Dr. Besant in the wood-lined living room of Arya Vihara. I was greatly impressed by her, but in a different way than at the Philharmonic. Here, in the privacy of her home, she was the embodiment of gentleness and graciousness. I was enchanted by a soft, feminine quality that emanated from her, in sharp contrast to the regal, austere style of her public personality. We sat down and spoke at length. She told me that Krishnaji had spoken to her about me, and she seemed very much interested in my Costa Rican background, my family's role in founding the Theosophical Society in that country, my school work and my plans for the future. When I rose to say goodbye, I felt like hugging her, there was such a genuinely sweet and motherly quality about her. Well could I understand Krishnaji's devotion to her.

Dr. Besant left for Europe some weeks later. Krishnaji, Rajagopal and I returned to the Philharmonic Auditorium soon afterward, this time to hear a talk by the British socialist John Strachey. We sat in the same box seats we had occupied for Dr. Besant's lecture, and that was the only similarity between the two events. Speaking in a monotone, Strachey marshaled a whole array of political and economic statistics in predicting the demise of the capitalist system, getting scattered applause along the way. Frankly, a lot of it was over my head, even though I was then sympathetic to the aims of socialism. Krishnaji was plainly bored, and I remember Rajagopal making some funny, caustic remark about Strachey's baggy pants and generally unkempt appearance, which sent Krishnaji into muffled chuckles as he tried to keep a straight face.

Driving home from the Philharmonic that evening, Krishnaji told me of an offer General Motors had recently made to him: they would give him a brand-new Cadillac of his choice if he allowed them to use his name and picture in posters all over the country endorsing the Cadillac. He thought the whole thing was a great joke and laughed about it.

I had been seeing Krishnaji on an average of twice a week when he stayed in Hollywood at the home of John Ingleman on Beachwood Drive. We talked, or we went to a show, or he came over to have dinner with my family. Then there were times, before his annual departure for Europe or India, when I couldn't seem to get to him. He was busy interviewing people, meeting the press, dictating letters. My usual personal problems, the kind most young people are afflicted with, had become aggravated at this time. I felt it imperative to talk to Krishnaji, but I couldn't seem to reach him. Finally I got him directly on the phone. He said to come right over. I did.

As always, Krishnaji appeared serene, happy, carefree. On that day, his peaceful spiritual aura had a strange effect on me: it irked me. Misery demands company. I sat next to him on the couch and excitedly protested that nothing was working out for me. Life was a "drag." He remained silent. Of course, he probably couldn't understand someone with real problems, I went on, for his life had always been smooth sailing. He had everything everybody wanted: money, fame, friends, independence, the freedom to do what he wanted most, and all this without ever having made any effort to get it; it had all been handed to him on a silver platter ever since he was a boy. Where would he be today if it hadn't been for Dr. Besant and her rich and influential friends? What did he know about loneliness, fear, unrequited love, boredom? I was trying hard to get a rise out of him, but the more I tried the more I got a sickening sensation of just punching the air, a very empty feeling that finally put a stop to my diatribe.

When I had gotten it all out of my system, he put a gentle hand on my knee and silently gazed at me. Suddenly I had the disconcerting feeling of something having been punctured inside of me, and all the hot air going out. After a long moment he said, "That's a great case you built against me, Sidney," a remark which made me feel like a boor and an ass. I realized the whole display had been a meaningless, childish outburst, uncalled for and rude. Then he added, "Why don't you try to come over to my side of the fence?"

I said I wished I could, but it seemed impossible. We talked a while longer. I apologized for my rude behavior, and he brushed it lightly aside. I'm sure it never touched him. That was precisely why I felt like such an idiot.

The following week I saw Krishnaji again at Star Head-quarters on Beachwood Drive. I had gone there to translate some letters into Spanish, and he sauntered in to see Rajagopal about something. He asked me then if I would like to accompany him and Rajagopal to see Eugene O'Neill's play *Lazarus Laughed* at the Pasadena Playhouse the following week. I happily accepted. From friends of the family in the movie industry, I learned that this was not one of O'Neill's great plays, but that Irving Pichel, the Shakespearean actor who was playing the lead, would make it worthwhile. For me, the important thing was that I would be sitting next to Krishnaji. Also, it would be a good opportunity to get to know Rajagopal better.

The evening of the play Rajagopal was in one of his witty, amusing moods. We laughed at his jokes and his acid remarks about some of Krishnaji's more emotional devotees. Rajagopal was a personable, good-looking young man of considerable charm who had recently graduated from Cambridge University and had come to Krishnaji with high spiritual credentials from one of the most prominent Theosophical leaders, C. W. Leadbeater. Krishnaji had appointed him General Secretary of the Order of the Star, a position that Nitya had held before his death, and he had proceeded to reorganize the entire organization. He was a good organizer and a hard worker. He was also very bossy and could be inflexible and petty in his work rules—the very opposite of Krishnaji. Having taken over the Order of the Star (which later became Krishnamurti Writings, Inc.), he ran the show with a firm hand.

This was a period of relative harmony between Krishnaji and Rajagopal. But even then, I sensed an undercurrent of jealousy in Rajagopal toward Krishnaji. It was clear to me that the bright Cambridge graduate resented playing a secondary role. But no one, of course, suspected that eventually an open break would occur.

Krishnaji, Rajagopal and I had dinner together and then drove out to Pasadena in Rajagopal's car. After the outburst of a few days previously, I was wonderfully relaxed and happy. It was always great fun to be with Krishnaji when you felt no need to discuss anything serious and could indulge in pleasant chatter and jokes. He loved good jokes, especially those that punctured fat egos, and was always enormously amused at the silly things people would say about the World Teacher. He laughed like a boy, in sudden outbursts of pure fun.

As I had never seen or read *Lazarus Laughed*, I didn't know what to expect. Neither Krishnaji nor Rajagopal knew anything about the play either, but we agreed that if it got overly pretentious we'd leave. Even then Krishnamurti had a low tolerance for the tenets of any organized religion.

During the intermission there was nothing said about leaving. We were very glad to return to our seats and hear again Irving Pichel's marvelously vibrant laughter whenever Lazarus, having just returned from the dead, was asked to tell about God. It was a laughter that filled the auditorium like music, saying different things to different people. It gave you goose pimples.

On the way home, we talked about the play. I thought it had been an inspiring performance. It had touched me deeply, not so much by the words, which sometimes had great power, as by the extraordinary quality of Lazarus's laughter. Krishnaji, who was not particularly a drama buff, seemed impressed. He said something about the deep truth of the play's main thesis: that no human being can formulate thoughts about God, so there is no recourse but to respond with laughter.

I drove him back to Arya Vihara the following day. It was a beautiful spring afternoon, and Krishnaji spoke glowingly of the beauty of the green hills, the lone tree standing by the road, the drifting clouds, a bird in flight. "You say you have attained to the basic unity of life," I said. "Does that mean that you know exactly what it means to be a bird in flight?"

He thought for a moment and said, "It's not quite like that. Because I know real beauty, I understand the significance and special beauty of a bird in flight." He went on to say that while watching the different manifestations of Nature you don't become "a bird in flight," or a "tree by the roadside," or a "drifting cloud." But because you have touched the real source of Beauty, Nature reveals its inner beauty to you. Then, to bring the conversation around to a problem that was bothering me, I asked if it worked the same way with people: in other words, did people reveal themselves to him as they were, with all their ugliness, their problems and their good things? "It's not the same thing," he answered. At this point I asked him point-blank about my problem.* As I spoke about it, I was aware of how childish and silly it sounded. That it amused Krishnaji didn't surprise me. But I felt that from the mountaintop where he dwelt, some of the petty problems that worried human beings didn't really concern him. And that irked me. He told me how to tackle the problem, but I felt his answer was inadequate and superficial, and I was disappointed and angry. However, some years later I asked him the same question, and with great patience and comprehen-

---

* Sidney carried the burden of one childhood event from Costa Rica with him all his life. He and his younger brother, Gilbert, were playing outside when the branch of a tree broke off and killed Gilbert. Sidney always felt responsible for his brother's death, yet he could never discuss this deeply painful episode with his father. Late in life he wrote a story called "The Shadow of the Tree." This might be the problem he discussed with Krishnamurti, who also had a special tie with his brother.

sion of the situation at its deepest level, he told me how to proceed. I followed his advice and realized what a master psychologist he is. He had given me the golden key to the problem. It was like opening a large window into a stuffy and airless room.

Before reaching Arya Vihara, I asked Krishnaji about sex. "I've heard so many different opinions about your views on the subject," I said.

"Forget about what you've heard," he returned, "and think of sex simply as energy, energy to be used to attain a goal." He knew I played a great deal of tennis and asked, "Would you indulge in sex prior to a tennis match?" I said no, not if I wanted to win. "That's just the point," he said quickly. "If you want to climb a mountaintop you conserve every ounce of energy."

"Does that mean a man who would attain the highest must be an ascetic?"

"Not at all. Asceticism as a goal is destructive. There is the biological need for sex, and there is also the need to conserve energy in order to attain a goal."

I knew Krishnaji had met D. H. Lawrence, a great literary favorite of mine at the time, and I asked him if he had read a recent interview published in the *Los Angeles Times* in which Lawrence said that in his opinion liberation was only possible momentarily through sex. Krishnaji laughed. Then he was pensively silent for a moment. "Liberation is sex inverted," he said.

"What do you mean?" I asked, perplexed.

"Think about it," he answered, a half smile on his lips. I'm still thinking about it.

4

KRISHNAJI WAS SOON LEAVING FOR EUROPE AND THE CAMP gathering at Ommen in Holland, in June 1928, so my family invited him, Rajagopal and Rosalind Williams, who had been staying at Arya Vihara, to come for a visit. This was the first time the family had met Rosalind. A beautiful girl, blonde and blue-eyed, she had a guileless quality about her that was very attractive. We all liked her.

It was a very pleasant social evening. One thing stands out from it clearly in my mind: Krishnaji asked my father whether, following my graduation from Hollywood High, he would let me go with him to the forthcoming Camp gathering at Ommen, and the pre-Camp gathering at Castle Eerde. The family was obviously pleased by this request, and I was thrilled.

Krishnaji was leaving in a few days, and I couldn't get myself ready that soon, so it was decided that I would go by myself as soon as my passport came through and arrangements were made for steamship passage. This took longer than expected, since it happened to be the start of the summer tourist rush to Europe. The delay worked in my favor, for it gave me a chance to attend a series of fun farewell parties given me by school friends.

It was all very exciting. I had never been away from my family, and I had never visited Europe. A great adventure—but also a little scary.

Finally the day of departure arrived. Accompanied by the whole family and some friends, I was bid farewell at the Southern Pacific station in Los Angeles, where the prestigious Sunset Limited train would take me to Chicago. (Airplanes were crossing the country, but they carried only mail and the occasional intrepid solo flier out to establish a new distance record.) In Chicago I was met by friends who put me on board the Century Limited to New York. I had been in New York three years before, when we had arrived from Costa Rica on our way to Hollywood, and I had loved it; but then there had been so many parental do's and don't's. This time there was no one to tell me what to do, where not to go, when to come in at night. After two days of freedom, a little confused and bewildered by the great city, I anxiously stepped on board the great cruise ship *Rotterdam*, flagship of the Holland American Line, and departed for Holland.

Five days later, after a smooth sailing with a festive crowd, I arrived at Rotterdam, a tremendously busy port city with masses of bicyclists on every street. A taxi took me directly to the railroad station, where I boarded a train for Amsterdam. I rode through flat, beautifully cultivated country of blazing poppy fields—crimson, white, yellow, pink—and arrived a couple of hours later. With some friends I had met en route, I went on a boat trip through one of the city's picturesque canals. I fell in love with Amsterdam immediately and wished I could stay there a few days. However, I had promised Krishnaji I'd go directly to Ommen, so I called Castle Eerde to say I would take the five o'clock train. Krishnaji's liveried chauffeur met me at the little Ommen station in the official Mercedes Benz convertible, and we drove on to Castle Eerde.

It was a misty evening when we arrived at the Castle Eerde estate. I shall never forget it. We drove slowly through a wide avenue of tall, magnificent beech trees, their heavy tops swaying gently, forming a whispering canopy overhead as they reached playfully toward each other in the mists. The tunnel of luscious, velvety greens framed the dim outline of the eighteenth-century castle at the far end, a scene reminiscent of a Walt Disney fantasy of the enchanted entrance to the legendary abode of Prince Charming.

The ornate wrought-iron gates were opened, and we were about to drive in when the chauffeur stopped the car to let a wandering deer leisurely cross the road. The deer looked at us curiously and trotted off. The chauffeur explained that Krishnaji had given orders that the deer in the woods had the right of way. The unexpected pause gave me a chance to get a first view of the great old castle at just the right distance. It stood serenely, in all its dignified splendor, facing the formal lawn and gardens, surrounded by a wide moat that was spanned by a broad, elegant bridge leading up to the stately entrance. The castle, together with its five thousand acres of surrounding woods and meadows, had been given to Krishnaji by Baron Phillip van Pallandt, a wealthy Dutch aristocrat and devoted friend.

I suppose I expected Krishnaji to meet me on arrival, or at least to be greeted by someone with a smile and a cheerful word. No one was around. The chauffeur showed me to my room in the annex, a new wing that had recently been built to accommodate guests. Presently, a Mrs. Christie came to meet me with the unwelcome news that I was one of the first guests to arrive. I asked to see Krishnaji. Instead, Lady Emily Lutyens appeared.* She seemed to be in charge of things, and although cool and aloof, with the appearance of a Victorian matron, she had an old-world charm that was very appealing. She informed me that Krishnaji had arrived the previous day from London with a bad cold and would be unable to see anyone for several days. Tough luck for me, I thought: I should have stayed in Amsterdam for a few days, as I had wanted to, playing tourist with some of my traveling companions. Still, I was here, in this fabulous place, with Krishnaji, whom I would probably see in a couple of days. Women were always overly protective of him because of his childlike innocence and magnetism. Meantime there would be books to read and records to play.

After a quiet dinner in the large, formal dining room with its elegant decor, I wandered around the place, admiring the priceless antique furniture, paintings, ancestral tap-

---

* The wife of the famous architect Sir Edwin Lutyens, she was one of the closest devotees of the young Krishnamurti; her daughter Mary became his official biographer.

estries and objets d'art. It was a magnificent place, regal yet unpretentious, truly befitting its master.

By the time I returned to my room, it had started to rain. Suddenly I felt terribly alone, thousands of miles away from my home and family. The next few days were most depressing. It rained continuously. One couldn't even go out for a walk through the beautiful woods because the paths were a series of impassable puddles. The few arrivals were older people who seemed to disappear into their rooms to "meditate and commune with the higher levels." The whole thing was a terrific comedown from the last few weeks of partying and fun. I presumed this period of "quiet introspection," as it was put to me, was a necessary prelude to the spiritual experiences ahead, so there seemed to be nothing to do but stick it out.

One evening I cornered Lady Emily after supper and asked her about Krishna's health. When would I be able to see him? "Whenever he's ready," she replied sternly. "And by the way," she went on, "now that Krishna has attained complete union with the World Teacher, it has been decided that we should all address him as Krishnaji, not just Krishna." She went on to explain the meaning of the "ji" after the name Krishna—an honorific term of affection and respect. I thought this was a good way of putting people on pedestals, something I knew Krishnaji detested. Why hadn't Sri Krishna been called Sri Krishnaji?

At any rate, Krishnaji remained incommunicado. The weather worsened. The books I might have read were under lock and key in the castle, and the record player was not to be used except with Rajagopal's permission, and he hadn't arrived yet.

Some of the younger camp guests started to arrive, mostly girls. This, unfortunately, didn't liven things up for

45

me, for there was an aura of spiritual snobbery about them which was hard to penetrate. They had been together at past gatherings and tended to be clannish and condescending toward a stranger.

I made up my mind to leave, at least for a few days. Quietly, without telling anyone, I could make a quick trip to Paris, have some fun there and return before anyone had even noticed my absence. It was an exciting idea. I called a travel agency in Ommen. They arranged for train tickets and reserved a room for me in a little hotel in Paris, L'Hôtel des États Unis. I was to leave the following day from Ommen, and I knew that for a small consideration I could get the friendly old chauffeur to drive me to the station and keep quiet about it.

That afternoon the sky cleared and the sun shone for the first time in ten days. But that was not the only reason why this day was to be of special significance. Sitting in my room, which overlooked the entrance to the castle, I was watching the welcome sunlight play through the treetops when suddenly I noticed a tall, slender girl, dressed in a long, clinging, black house robe splashed with huge red roses, crossing the lawn on her way to the castle. She walked with an easy, swinging stride, full of self-confidence, as if she were giving the party herself. Her long hair was jet black, and the red rose she wore in it matched those on her robe. She was the brightest and most joyously alive sight I had seen since my arrival ten days earlier, and she seemed close to me in age. I was immediately intrigued and decided I must meet her then and there. I quickly combed my hair, dashed out and sat excitedly on the bridge's rampart, waiting for her to come out of the castle. Suddenly she was standing before me. We both smiled and said hello. Then I said something inconsequential about the fine weather after so much rain, and introduced myself.

"My name is Ruth Roberts," she said with a pleasing English accent. "Aren't you the American boy?"

"Yes. How did you know? Are you clairvoyant?" She laughed, a warm, husky laughter, which I liked right away.

"I read the guest list." Then she added, "But you don't sound like an American."

I explained I had been born in Costa Rica, and she immediately responded that she liked my accent, which I thought I had gotten rid of. She sat down beside me, and we talked for some time. She had a haughty kind of beauty, luminous black eyes with a mischievous spark to them and an air of independence that encouraged me to speak my mind. I had not mentioned my plan to go to Paris the following day, but she sensed my great disappointment in not being able to see Krishnaji.

"You're a fool to bank on Krishnaji," she said, matter-of-factly.

She was right. Krishnaji himself had warned me about it. But there it was, and I didn't like the feeling of it. She walked away with a teasing smile, and I watched her sensuously feline movements as she disappeared into the women's section of the annex.

I felt an instant attraction to her, but never for a moment imagined that later on my life would be linked with hers. She had been charming, but it was obvious that she regarded me as a kid. I wavered in my decision to go off to Paris the following day, yet I worried about the immature image I had projected. Perhaps if I went to Paris, even for a few days, she might regard me as a more sophisticated person on my return. I kept remembering the words of my French teacher at Hollywood High, who used to say, "Paris will make a man out of you." I was preoccupied with these thoughts when Lady Emily appeared with the news that Krishnaji would see me tomorrow afternoon at three. That did it. Paris, for the time being, was forgotten. But not Ruth.

I was so excited about seeing Krishnaji that I hardly slept that night. I was also hurt about the long silence and made up my mind to be cool, aloof and distant, and to let him know how I had felt these past ten days.

The next day I knocked at his door on the second floor of the castle promptly at three. My heart was beating fast when I heard his voice asking me to come in. To judge by Lady Emily's previous reports regarding his condition, I expected Krishnaji to be pale, thin and haggard. But the man I saw as I opened the door, sitting cross-legged on a low dais, clothed in a golden robe over his white dhoti, was the most radiant, beautiful human being I had ever seen. He literally took my breath away as I stood, immobile, gazing at him. It was an unforgettable moment. He smiled and said, "Come in, come in, Sidney," and motioned for me to sit on the dais alongside him. I advanced tentatively, and, overwhelmed with emotion, sat beside him. Out of politeness I wanted to ask about his health, although he certainly had never looked healthier since I had known him, but I was unable to say a word.

After a long silence he said he was aware that I had been unhappy. I nodded. He went on to say it was inevitable I should feel let down after my social activity of the last few weeks. I wondered how he knew about that, as I hadn't seen him or communicated with him for over two months, but I figured it was a reasonable assumption. His eyes were particularly luminous as he gazed at me. Then he said, "I'm glad you canceled your trip to Paris." This really startled me, as I had not told anyone about my plans. "Paris is a beautiful city, but it's a rotten hole," he added. When I found my tongue, I said I intended to visit it after the Camp.

Walter J. Field, Sidney's father.

Sidney at about 12, in Costa Rica.

The Field family house in Hollywood until 1939.

Left to right: Sidney's sisters Lolita and Flora, his mother Cinta, and Sidney, in front of their house in Hollywood.

Sidney as the young head of the family.

Krishnamurti in the 1920's.

J. Krishnamurti

K. in his teens in India.

Sidney with girlfriend
and car.

Sidney as the young head of
the family.

Sidney welcomes K. to Hollywood High.

Profile of Krishnamurti in 1936.

Krishnamurti in Hollywood: visiting the set of *King of Kings* (1927), one of the last silent films. Victor Varconi, the Hungarian-born star, is dressed as Pontius Pilate on the left, and director Cecil B. DeMille stands on the right.

The conversation then drifted to the beauties of the castle and the estate, which he promised to show me personally in a few days, when we would go for a long walk through the woods and pastures. There was another long silence, which I felt was an invitation to discuss my problems. But at that moment there were no problems of any sort. I felt a great peace and contentment. The visit was at an end. As I got up to go, he told me that almost all the guests had arrived and that tomorrow morning he would give a short welcoming talk in the library.

At eleven o'clock the following morning, we all assembled in the spacious library and sat on a beautiful Persian rug facing Krishnaji, who sat cross-legged on a sofa, the only piece of furniture left in the room, under one of the magnificent seventeenth-century Gobelin tapestries made expressly for the castle. He started his talk by saying that we had all been together with him in past lives and would be together with him in future lives. (I mentioned this remark to him recently and he said, very surprised, "Did I say that?") It was a short talk in which he briefly outlined what he wanted to do in the world: to set men free, to help them stand on their own feet, free of all authority.

At some point during the talk, something extraordinary happened to me. For no apparent reason I experienced a sudden outburst of intense joy in the region of the heart. It went on and on in increasingly strong rhythmic waves, until I thought I would have to open my mouth and shout for joy. I was reminded of Irving Pichel's laughter in *Lazarus Laughed*—only this was the real thing, uninvited, unsought, possessing my entire being. It was an experience that practically lifted me out of my body, something I had never felt before or thought I could ever feel.

After the talk most of the guests took advantage of the

sun-drenched morning and went out into the woods for a short walk before lunch. I stayed by myself, hoping to preserve the fragrance of that indescribable moment as long as possible. Alone and undisturbed under the leafy shade of a tall elm, I felt the joyous force quieting down to the rhythm of my breathing, bringing with it a sense of great peace and up-welling love. As the days passed, it receded into the background. I looked forward to my forthcoming walk with Krishnaji in the hope that he might be able to ignite again the inner spark that had given me such a great high a few days before. I longed to be swept up again in that joyous flame that had made the world appear purified and innocent, as if it had just come into being that morning.

We did go for a walk, Krishnaji and I, but the longed-for experience did not happen. Nevertheless, there was a wonderful feeling of lightness, clarity and serenity. We walked leisurely, and mostly silently, under the big trees and over seldom trod dirt paths, where brightly colored butterflies darted in and out of light and shadow. Krishnaji seemed intensely aware of every changing mood of Nature, of every living thing around, even the bugs under foot, which he was careful not to step on. I told him that I thought he had given an inspiring talk when he welcomed his guests, but never said a word about the spiritual experience I had undergone. It was too new, too fragile to discuss, like a tender plant that must be carefully nourished and not exposed to any strong wind. I felt I must tend it with my own hands, uninfluenced by anyone. I had previously experienced the way Krishnaji, at the least expected moment, would drop a casual remark that packed all the force of a Caribbean hurricane, wiping you out. I was taking no chances.

Just the same, I skirted around the subject, anxious to

get his viewpoint on a matter of such vital importance to me. "Before you attained your goal of Liberation,"* I asked, "did you have any special experiences, like . . . well, a great sense of joy and freedom?"

"Yes," he answered.

"What did you do about it?"

"Nothing. I never pursued such experiences."

"But if you felt that such an experience was an important signpost along the way, did you encourage it?"

"I looked at it with great awareness, with affection, to find out where it was leading."

That was a satisfying answer, and I was content to leave it at that.

Visitors came daily to visit Krishnaji at the castle. Some would stay for a few hours, others for two or three days. Among them, on a brief visit, were two of the "Apostles" announced a year earlier to help the World Teacher spread his teaching. The Apostles were proclaimed by a leading English Theosophist, the flamboyant George Arundale, who included himself among their number. He also appointed his wife, Rukmini Devi, a beautiful young Brahmin woman, who, together with Bishop James Wedgwood, was also one of the visitors to the castle. Rukmini was lovely in her colorful Indian sari. She was open and friendly, and everyone liked her. Bishop Wedgwood, tall and darkly handsome in his ecclesiastic vestments, wearing a large, bejewelled pectoral cross and episcopal ring, appeared rather forbidding among the easygoing guests at the castle. He was standoffish, filled with a sense of his own importance, and he reeked of spiritual arrogance. I had a

* In Krishnamurti's philosophy, the central tenet of Liberation came to mean an inner freedom attained when a person has been able to detach himself or herself from emotional, psychological and physical dependence of any kind.

letter of introduction to him from a good friend of mine who knew him well, but I was so completely put off I didn't bother to hand it to him.

Krishnaji had been very much upset by the absurd and sensational announcements made by George Arundale and Bishop Wedgwood to the effect that certain people had been chosen to be "Krishnaji's Apostles." Arundale claimed the message had come from the Lord Maitreya. Krishnaji angrily rejected the whole business, stating he had no disciples of any kind. Those who knew how disgusted he felt privately about it were surprised at the moderation with which he handled the matter in public, not aware that his love for Dr. Besant, who had been drawn into it through her trust in Arundale, prevented him from doing anything drastic that might embarrass her or hurt her feelings. (Years later, however, in Ojai, he expressed himself very strongly on the subject, stating that both Arundale and Wedgwood had ruthlessly tried to use him to aggrandize themselves. I discussed the subject with him personally and know how outraged he was at the methods they used to further their own ends.)

The long summer days slipped happily into weeks. There were more walks with Krishnaji through the lovely woods, and several informal talks when nothing revealing or profound was said because there seemed to be no need for anything except being there and enjoying his company.

The last talk I had with him, however, was disturbing. I had just graduated from high school before coming to Eerde, and although I had never been particularly devoted to schooling, I did intend to go on to college. All I needed was a little encouragement. I didn't get it from Krishnaji. When I asked him if I should continue with my education and pursue a career, he responded with the same sentiments he had expressed in previous talks with me: that the only important thing in life was to learn to be inwardly free, unconditionally free, to attain liberation. Everything else was a waste of time. "Do not waste your time. Every day counts. Set your goal and concentrate all your energy in realizing it," he said again and again, his whole personality afire with the personal goal he had set for himself, to set all men free.

To forget about education and a career and become "liberated" was not the best advice to give to an impressionable boy just beginning to open his eyes to a new world. This counsel, I suppose, was in line with Krishnaji's views and feeling about the world then, but to judge by his views on education later in life, I very much doubt he would have continued to recommend it. Through the years there were changes in Krishnaji's technique of communication and his manner of conveying his teaching, which, generally speaking, appeared much sharper and more lucid in his later years. Perhaps he himself foresaw this many years ago when I said to him, after one of his early talks, that I had not understood what he was trying to say, that it was too choppy and disconnected. He answered, "Yes, I muffed it this morning. I'm trying to say something about a new dimension, to convey new meanings, but my words are interpreted in the old way. Like a painter expressing something new, I'm learning a new technique. It's not easy." He paused for a moment and then added. "But wait until I'm sixty . . ." At any rate, I didn't want to let our exchange about my future cast a shadow over the wonderful experience that Eerde had been, so I temporarily put it out of my mind.

Lazy, contemplative days followed, as well as exciting, fun days. There was rowing around the picturesque moat surrounding the castle, and there were games, mostly volleyball, in which Krishnaji sometimes took part. There was the fun of making friends with interesting people from many lands,* and the challenge of self-discoveries. I felt immensely grateful to Krishnaji for having given me the opportunity of being there with him, a sentiment which was hard to convey to him, for he refused to have anyone beholden to him. At all times he radiated a spiritual quality that sharpened one's awareness and sensitivity.

During this time I did not see much of my exciting new friend, Ruth Roberts. She was generally busy with her own, older friends. Among them was a wealthy Dutch philosopher, J. J. Van der Leeuw, about ten years her senior, who had proposed marriage. Koos, as everyone called him, was a very tall man, and very serious, as philosophers are apt to be. In addition, he was totally bald. And thereby hangs a little tale, one which the erudite philosopher never tired of telling. It appears that one sunny afternoon he was innocently standing right under the second-story window of one of the bedrooms in the annex when suddenly he felt a blob of gooey matter drop on his bald pate. Philosopher that he was, he remained calm and collected, thinking some large passing bird had zeroed in on him and discharged. It was his karma; he would make the best of it. Slowly and with a minimum of fuss, so as to remain unnoticed, he reached for his head to remove the dropping. Then the truth dawned upon him. The offending stuff was ordinary toothpaste. A dirty trick perpetuated by someone with a warped

---

* In its heyday the Theosophist Society attracted prominent and wealthy people, some of whom built permanent cabins at the camp. During the summer of 1928, visitors to Ommen included the conductor Leopold Stokowski and his wife; Sir Roderick Jones, the head of Reuters, and his wife; the writer Enid Bagnold; and several members of Parliament from England.

sense of humor, he figured. Full of righteous anger, he looked up, and, according to his own report, saw Krishnaji and Rajagopal hiding behind a window directly above him, teetering with laughter. Koos unburdened himself of some choice expletives and headed for the nearest shower. The theme of Liberation had been carried too far!

Later, and in fun, I asked Krishnaji if he or Rajagopal were responsible for squeezing the toothpaste tube with such deadly accuracy on Koos's bald head. Krishnaji laughed with mischievous exuberance and said simply that Rajagopal had a quaint sense of humor, adding that Koos was too straitlaced about the whole thing.

The happy days at Castle Eerde came to an end too soon. The guests started packing, ready to move on to the Camp grounds, within the estate, about a mile from the castle.

It had rained early, clearing in the late afternoon, when Krishnaji and I went for a walk in the woods. The sky was streaked with color and summer light, and the ground under our feet was redolent of brown leaves and damp earth. We walked in silence for some time. The thought that I would probably never see this extraordinary place again cast a shadow of sadness over me. I tried to recall some of the more significant and special moments of my memorable stay there. Instead, a kaleidoscope of unrelated, inconsequential events flashed through my mind: Krishnaji walking alone through the woods, sporting his new black beard and looking frighteningly Christlike. Lady Emily agitatedly asking me to talk in Spanish to one of the guests, a prominent gentleman from Puerto Rico, and ask him to please abstain from spitting when he went out for a walk. (The culprit spat in rapid succession from each side of the mouth with great force and purpose, as if intent on setting

some kind of record.) "It's most antiesthetic and unsani-
tary," Lady Emily complained. A young student from London stripping and plunging naked into the old moat to
retrieve the volley ball we had been playing with, while the
other startled players giggled nervously. A visitor from
C. W. Leadbeater's manor in Sydney, Australia, excitedly
explaining that he couldn't understand what Krishnaji was
talking about because he was not a "bodhisattva man." Tall,
fun-loving Ruth striding along a wooded path with a dash-
ing army captain from California, while "the American boy
from Costa Rica," as I had come to be known, looked on
forlornly.

I knew I was not likely to see Krishnaji during the
Camp Ommen lectures, so I said goodbye to him as we
stood for a moment by the main gate to the castle. I said a
few words of gratitude that seemed entirely inadequate and
gave him an *abrazo*, or Latin embrace. He did likewise, told
me how much he had enjoyed having me there, and said
that we would be seeing more of each other later on. That
was the cue that released again that wonderful burst of
joyous laughter, lifting me to the treetops and leaving me
speechless. Fortunately, I had already said goodbye, so I
just walked away into the woods. It was dusk when I returned to my room in the annex. Everyone had already left.

While I waited outside for the chauffeur to return and
pick me up, I reflected upon that great joyous gift, the
spiritual legacy of my trip to Castle Eerde, and made up my
mind that this time I would not lose it. But I was to learn, in
time, that this was not the kind of experience you make up
your mind to have, on command. It was a totally sponta-
neous thing that happened, or didn't happen, and could not
be invited, coaxed or cajoled. But at the time it was a great
beginning to the Camp session and, to me, the most impor-

tant thing about the proceedings. I remember, too, how Krishnaji's fireside chanting in Sanskrit was always delightful, his voice melting with the crackling fire and soaring upward with the dancing flames.

The Camp ended, and I went off to Belgium and Paris. Paris was beautiful and exciting. The seamy side of it, which Krishnaji had warned me about, was something you could get close to without getting burned.

5

BEFORE LEAVING EERDE, I HAD RECEIVED A LETTER FROM MY parents asking me to call on the Tinocos while in Paris. Mrs. Tinoco had written Mother to say they had heard I was at the Ommen Camp and that they wanted to see me and get the latest news of Krishnamurti. Tinoco had by this time lost all his ill-gotten money; he was ill and living in a garret. With some difficulty I found their small, second-story apartment in the Latin Quarter, but they were not home. A neighbor told me that Tinoco had been taken to the hospital a few days previously, gravely ill, and that Mrs. Tinoco was staying with friends. The former Costa Rican strongman was penniless, the neighbor said, and gaunt with old age. He had been eking out a living by meeting the luxury liners at Cherbourg, wrapped in his black and red cape, his Andalusian hat at a jaunty angle, and inviting rich American tourists, always alert for the bizarre, on a guided tour of Paris for a nominal sum.

A few days after my visit, the legendary Federico Tinoco died—the man who had dreamed of building a society based on Krishnamurti's teachings; the man who had been enthusiastically welcomed to power by his fellow citizens, only to be feared and hated by them in the end; the man who had shown such gentle patience in teaching a small boy how to pronounce the words in *At the Feet of the Master*.

From Paris I went to London. Krishnaji had spoken enthusiastically about the English capital, his second home, so I was looking forward to exploring it. But I found the city, although historically exciting, personally unfriendly. After some weeks there, I was glad to board the Cunard liner *Olympic,* at Southampton, for the voyage back to the States. I found the Arundales on board and saw a good deal of them during the trip and later in Hollywood. Rukmini, as on my first meeting with her, was charming and relaxed. "Apostle" George was something else. He gave one the impression of being a highly competent man, and would probably have made an excellent corporate vice president. He had charm and magnetism, and was an excellent raconteur and a born actor. Indeed, the stage might have been his real vocation. He loved surprise entrances and dramatic postures, and hated being upstaged. The role of Right Reverend, into which he had recently cast himself, he played to the hilt, but you couldn't take him seriously as the spiritual leader he pretended to be.

Paris, London, New York, Chicago—they were exciting and fun for a young man embarking upon life, but hardly the appropriate ground upon which to cultivate that rare spiritual flower I had found at Eerde, which now seemed a faraway dream. I boarded the Sunset Limited in Chicago on my way back to Hollywood, depressed and discouraged, wondering whether I would ever again touch that deep and purifying force.

One day I was standing against the side railing in the open section of the observation car, traveling fast through the New Mexico desert. I was not thinking about anything in particular, just taking in the vast monotony of the desert scene, hot and dusty, when a giant sunflower growing beside the railroad tracks, a few inches from destruction, brushed rapidly past my face, incredibly close, its golden face momentarily shutting out the world. Like a coiled spring, the great Joy, self-exiled these past few weeks, leaped out of me, as if to greet the daring flower beside the railroad tracks—a joyous sunburst to the glorious sunflower!

The train sped on as I watched the magnificent bloom slowly fade and disappear in the distance. Outwardly nothing had changed. The same dull, fat people still sat in the observation car, watching the same hot, dusty desert. Yet, miraculously, everything had changed for me. The heightened awareness revealed a desert that was a marvel of beauty. The people around me, fat and ugly, had somehow acquired a quality I had not been aware of before, something, perhaps, deep down in them, that touched the life of the lovely flower they hadn't even noticed. Truly, it was a startling, marvelous experience, once more totally unexpected and uninvited. I wondered how long it would last. But I promised myself not to worry about that now.

I brought back with me a letter for my father, Krishnaji's response to my father's letter to him, which I had hand-delivered in Eerde. It pleased my father enormously:

June 19, 1927

My dear Mr. Field:

Thank you very much for your letter which you sent by Sidney. I am so glad to have him here, and I hope he will be happy too.

I am so glad that you have bought those fifteen acres just off the Star land at Ojai; but as we are so low financially, I am afraid we cannot at present buy the land from you, but if you will kindly keep it for some time with the idea of giving us the first option, I shall be very grateful. I am very glad that the land is in your hands, and not in some stranger's. As your land adjoins the Star land, it will be very useful to the Camp. I was and am eager to get it so as to round out the land; but as I said and as you know, we are very low financially, so I hope you will keep it for us and sell it to us at a later time.

I know Mr. Hall is very able in getting land for us all, and I am really very grateful to him for all the work he has done in connection with the Star land.

You will be hearing from Sidney of all our work here, and so I will not bother you with such things; but let me assure you how happy I am that I have your friendship.

Please give my love to John and to the family.

Sincerely and

affectionately

J. Krishnamurti

J. Krishnamurti

Krishnaji returned to Ojai the following year. He brought with him a close friend, Jadu Prasad, whom I had met at Eerde and liked very much. Jadu had an open, warm personality, a sharp mind and a delightful sense of humor.

Soon afterward, all the Arya Vihara crowd—Krishnaji, Rajagopal, Jadu and Rosalind—came over for dinner. Rosalind and Rajagopal had recently been married, so the occasion had a particularly festive meaning. It was a fun gathering, during which Krishnaji was greatly amused at an escapade of my brother, John. John had gone to a party with his favorite girlfriend, and despite Prohibition, he had drunk too much. A friend brought him home and he went to bed. Some time later he woke up, still under the influence, and realized that his girlfriend had remained at the party unescorted. Deciding to go to her immediately, he got out of bed, opened the window of his second-story bedroom and stepped right out! An awning under the window broke his fall, which, nevertheless, caused a deep cut in his head. When he came to, confused and disoriented, he proceeded to walk over to a neighbor's house across the street. He entered through the back door (in those days few houses were locked at night), went into the kitchen, took a piece of chicken out of the refrigerator and sat down to eat it. Awakened by the commotion, the Japanese house boy got up to investigate. As he entered the kitchen, he froze with fright at the sight of a strange man in pajamas, his face a bloody mess, calmly eating a piece of chicken. The boy screamed in terror. John fled, miraculously finding his way home. In the backyard he called to me, waking me up. I let him in, wondering whether I was dreaming. Meanwhile, the neighbors had called the police, who followed the trail of blood to our house and knocked loudly at the front door. We tried to persuade them that John was a sleepwalker who had mistaken the window for a door, but they insisted on seeing him. While my parents argued with the police, I rushed

upstairs to my brother's bedroom and coached him, ban-
daged and still dazed, on what to say to the police. Under
no circumstances must he admit that he was intoxicated.
When they finally saw him, his only response to them was,
"I am a sleepwalker. I am a sleepwalker." I don't think they
believed a word of it; his breath belied the story. But they
were good-natured about it, and simply warned him to
watch his step while sleepwalking.

During this time following Krishnamurti's return, I
was having to cope with new responsibilities. My father
had not been well, and my brother went off to Costa Rica.
Since my father had been unable to take care of his complicated business affairs personally, I had been elected to do
most of it myself. I had always hated the business world,
but I was in it now up to my neck. Meantime the great and
joyous laughter of Eerde had been reduced to an occasional
chuckle. It greatly worried and distressed me, although I
had come to the conclusion that I could do nothing but
hope eventually to come across another spectacular sunflower that touched the miracle button.

I drove to Ojai often to have lunch or dinner with
Krishnaji and his "family." We talked at length about my
difficult position and the great dissatisfaction in my life at
this stage, but there were no easy solutions, no pat answers.
There were, however, some interesting dinner table conver-
sations. At one of them Rajagopal asked Krishnaji point-
blank, "Is there, or is there not, reincarnation? Yes or no?"

Krishnaji thought for a moment and then said, "Reincarnation is a fact, but it's not true."

Seeing our startled reaction, he explained the apparent
contradiction in this way: "That which reincarnates is impermanent, and therefore not Truth, which is permanent
and everlasting."

There was also a Camp gathering at Ojai, which had been very well attended that year, but for some reason which I don't remember, it proved to be the last one. Henceforward, Krishnaji would hold weekend talks in the Oak Grove. Some of the people I had met at Eerde had come to Ojai for the Camp, including Ruth, who had in the meantime married John Tettemer, an extraordinary man some thirty-five years her senior who had spent most of his life as a monk in Rome. He shocked the Vatican when, as the youngest head of the Passionist Fathers, he left the church because he had lost his faith in the absolute truth of Catholicism. (He later published an account of his experience in a book, *I Was a Monk*.) The former priest had great warmth and vitality, and I liked him right away. He was very much interested in Krishnaji's teachings, which we often discussed, though Ruth, surprisingly, remained rather aloof from it all.

During this last Camp gathering I volunteered to bring Krishnaji's lunch, prepared on the Camp grounds, to Arya Vihara. It was always a problem to keep the soup from spilling during the five-mile trip by automobile. One day, as I handed him his tray, I asked him in jest, "Wouldn't this be much simpler if you could just levitate yourself over to the Camp and descend by the dining room?"

To my surprise, he said, quite seriously, "I have the key to all that, but I'm not interested."

I said it would be wonderful and most practical to have some of those powers. He responded with his usual affirmation that the only thing worth having was Liberation. To reinforce his point, he told me a little story about a great yogi he had known in India, who had developed all kinds of *siddhis* (powers acquired through meditation) and could do amazing things, which he had witnessed himself, such as levitating, rendering himself invisible, and growing plants from seeds in a few minutes. Before he left the yogi's home, the great magician said to him, "I would happily trade all my *siddhis* for a glimpse of Nirvana."

A rumor floated around the Camp grounds that Krishnaji had been given a large amount of cash by a friend. The rumor was totally groundless, but Rajagopal and Rosalind were very worried because they had heard footsteps outside at night. When I arrived at Arya Vihara one evening for my usual visit, I was met outside the house by Byron Casselberry, a young Theosophist who later became Rajagopal's assistant. Armed with a mean-looking iron poker, he was ready to crack my head open. He had not recognized my car in the darkness and was taking no chances. I went inside with him and met Rajagopal, armed with another poker. He said a Peeping Tom, or else a thief, had been seen outside just a few minutes before, and that Krishnaji had gone out into the orange grove to try to talk the man out of any mischief. I said that Krishnaji should not be left alone out there, and Rajagopal, who was very upset, replied that he was quite fed up with Krishnaji's "misplaced sympathy," and that he had already called the police.

I went out among the orange trees and found Krishnaji with a flashlight, looking for the culprit. I urged him to return indoors with me, saying the man might be violent. "I want to warn him to go away, that it's not worthwhile," he replied, and repeated, "It's not worthwhile." At that moment I could have hugged him. Here was this slight man, with nothing more lethal on his person than a small flashlight, alone in the dark, determined to warn a possibly violent character to flee before he was caught or set upon by Rajagopal and Byron. He continued his search with me for a while, then we both went indoors. Rajagopal met him with a barrage of harsh words, telling him that he had a talent for misplacing sympathy and that the trespasser should be dealt with severely. Krishnaji listened silently and, as he had done many times before when Rajagopal had become abusive, simply picked up his large Mexican hat and strode out.

Soon afterward, just prior to Krishnaji's departure for Europe, I was out at Arya Vihara again for lunch. Rosalind was very upset because the excellent vegetarian cook, a former Theosophist, had given notice that she was leaving. Krishnaji reminded her that the woman had taken the cooking job only to be near him. Once he was gone, what was the point in continuing to work in the Arya Vihara kitchen? Rosalind argued that she was well paid and well treated, and besides, there were other important people at Arya Vihara besides Krishnaji. He chuckled and took me by the arm to lead me into the kitchen, where we both helped the discerning cook do the dishes.

By this time, a few years after Eerde and a score of meaningless jobs in between, I had decided to disregard Krishnaji's advice about schooling and so entered UCLA. Before his departure, Krishnaji asked me to attend the Ommen Camp during the school vacation, but it was impossible for me to leave my family this time because of my father's delicate health. Some months later I heard that Krishnaji had had a bad case of food poisoning in Romania. I wrote him a long letter, which he promptly answered.

June 5, 1931

My dear Sidney,

Thank you very much for your letter, and I hope you do not mind my having the answer typewritten as I am rather busy just now and am trying to get ready to take a holiday before the Gathering.

67

As you have asked, I have been rather ill, but I am nearly allright now. I think it was some kind of poisoning in Roumania and it has lasted for a very long time. But I am getting better all the time.

I have been touring through Germany, Austria, England and Scotland, and returned here about a month ago. During this month of June I am going to stay in a hut in Camp and really rest before the Gathering and Camp begin.

I should love to see you, too, but I am afraid it cannot be done this year, as I am going to India, Java and Australia. I leave for India about the first of October, stopping in Greece where there is going to be a Gathering near Athens, then going on to Alexandria in Egypt and catching the boat at Port Said on the 21st. I will stay four months in India before going to Java and Australia. I hope to be in California about this time next year. I, also, should love to have a talk with you and I hope we shall have some nice times together when I come there.

I am so very glad Mr. Field is very much better and that Dr. Strong has done him good. Of course I can imagine he must be still very delicate but I hope, when I see him again next June, he will be completely well. Please give him my love and tell him I am looking forward with pleasure to seeing him again.

Give my love to John. I hope he has had a good time in Costa Rica and I hope, too, that he has not fallen out of the window!

I am glad the T. S.* is tightening up about me—I expect I shall presently be the Black Devil who is not mentioned at all in their sacred meetings. Good luck to them all!

[Krishnamurti added in his own hand]:

My dear Sidney, I am so glad you wrote to me and I hope you don't mind if my reply is typewritten. I have been thinking of you and your family so often and when I come to Cal. next June, I hope we shall have some fun together. I stay at the Camp [i.e., Ommen] in a hut and come here to the castle for my lunch and dinner. It's lovely here and I wish you were here too.

> With all my love yourself,
> Krishna.

> Please give my love to the family.

Two months later my father died of heart failure. Although not entirely unexpected, his passing was a great

---

* Theosophical Society, with which he had broken in 1929.

blow to me. I was suddenly catapulted into his role as head of the family, with endless problems and diminishing funds. I continued attending college and managed to finish my second year. But the pressures of being head of the family and student were getting too heavy. I quit, hoping always to return and complete my degree.

Some days after my father's death, Jadu Prasad, who had stayed on at Arya Vihara, died of a stroke. I had become very fond of Jadu and deeply felt his loss. I wrote Krishnaji then, and he quickly replied.

September 10, 1931

My dear Sidney,

I am so grieved to hear about your loss. I have thought of you all many times since and send you my love.

As you know, I will be in California the end of October, so I hope I shall have the pleasure of seeing you all.

It is really awful about Jadu. I can hardly believe that he is dead. I only received some days ago a letter from him in which he was very cheerful and enthusiastic about things. He will be a great loss as he was so intelligent and so enthusiastic.

Please give my love to the family and to John. Much love to yourself.

Yours affectionately,

Krishna

It was close to Christmas when Krishnaji returned to Ojai. On different occasions he had given me several beautiful ties. With his elegant, tailor-made suits he always wore the finest ties, chosen with exquisite taste, and every time I admired one of them he would immediately take it off and present it to me. It got to be embarrassing. I hated to think that he might feel that I admired his ties with ulterior motives. At any rate, I felt I should replace some of those ties, and while I didn't think I could match the quality and style of the ones he had given me, I sent him a couple of Italian silk imports I thought he might like. Some days later I received the following letter from him, which I thought charming for its directness and that unique quality of innocence that has always distinguished him.

Dec. 26th '31

My dear Sidney,

It was really very good of you to have sent me those two ties, which you really shouldn't have done as I am getting rid of things, but I shall keep them in friendship. Thank you so very much Sidney, I don't give presents but when you next come up here, you can have one of my ties. Thank you.

It has been cloudy and rainy since a week and all last night and this morning it has been pouring.

Please give my love and greetings to the family. I hope you are all having a happy Christmas and I wish you all a happy New Year.

Much love to you Sidney
Krishna.

6

AFTER MY FATHER'S DEATH, I WAS THROWN INTO A TURMOIL OF acrimonious legal battles to save the rapidly vanishing family estate. What had been saved from the sale of our Costa Rican coffee plantations had been held in trust by the Bank of America, which the family had to sue. It would take many years of frustration and mounting legal costs to win these battles. Here I was, at the threshold of adult life, just beginning the whole painful business, when Krishnaji kindly called me up to invite me to spend a week with him at Arya Vihara. Rosalind and Rajagopal were going to be away that week, and I'd have a chance to relax and be alone with him, to do anything I pleased. To be in Arya Vihara with Krishnaji, away from Hollywood and my sordid problems, loomed like a bit of paradise to me.

A pleasing warmth and the fragrance of orange blossoms filled the peaceful Ojai Valley the afternoon I arrived at Arya Vihara. Krishnaji was sitting alone on the front porch of his private cottage, behind the main house. There was a feeling of great peace and power about him. He said how happy he was that I had come. This remark presented an opportunity to ask him a question that had often come to mind. I said, "Krishnaji, does the presence of a friend, one you're fond of, make you happier than the presence of just anyone who might come in from the outside?"

His smile told me immediately that he knew the meaning of my question. He answered, "I am truly happy that you are here, Sidney, but if you hadn't come I'd be just as happy."

That took the wind out of my ego's sails, but after all, I reasoned, what else could he say and remain consistent with his view of complete self-sufficiency? He asked me how I was faring in Hollywood, and I gave him all the grim details of my court battles, with which he greatly sympathized. We then went for a long walk in the coolness of the late afternoon, behind the Thatcher School, in the shadow of the great Topa Topa mountain, enveloped in its darkening robe of dusk. All his life Krishnaji was a great lover of Nature, and it was always fun walking with him because you felt the bubbling sense of joy he experienced in the outdoors. As we tramped over the brush and rocks, I couldn't help but think of the remark he had made earlier in the day, pulling the rug out from under me, when I had asked him, indirectly, if he had any favorites. It was, perhaps, an impertinent question, for it was obvious that a man like Krishnaji was really not one of us, even if he was concerned about our problems and sorrows. He was a man alone, unentangled, unattached, living on the mountaintop like a solitary eagle.

After a delicious vegetarian dinner that evening, we went into the kitchen to help wash and dry the dishes, a chore that Krishnaji had imposed on himself to help the aging cook. Then we moved into the wood-paneled living room, where Krishnaji built a fire in the fireplace. Both of us sat on a couch, watching the fire without making a single comment. There is something wonderfully relaxing about dancing flames and crackling wood in a fireplace. Tonight, however, the psychic atmosphere in that charming old California bungalow, given to him by a friend, was not conducive to relaxation. The feeling was more like that generated by a giant dynamo. There was a powerful force concentrated there; it was almost physically palpable. It didn't surprise me, though, for many times before I had felt it in Krishnaji's presence, although never with such intensity.

Krishnaji was one of those rare persons who could be perfectly relaxed in the company of another while completely silent, and I had visions of spending the whole evening with him just watching the fire wordlessly. I kept thinking about a remark he had once made to me, that he was like a deep well, out of which each person took as much of the quenching spiritual waters as he was capable of drinking. Unfortunately, the highly charged atmosphere tonight had a curious effect on me. Instead of sharpening my sensitivity, it dulled it. Perhaps I had eaten too much. Whatever the cause, my usually meager capacity to drink from the Well of Wisdom had diminished alarmingly. I simply wasn't able to frame any kind of question appropriate to the occasion.

At length, Krishnaji got up to stoke the fire. He turned and faced me, straight and austere, regal in appearance, a prince in faded Levi's and worn cotton shirt, his expressive black eyes alight with a great fire. All at once, the veil of unawareness that had obscured my perceptions vanished. I felt entirely vulnerable.

"What do you want out of life, Sidney?"

"I'm not sure, Krishnaji. I thought I knew in Eerde, when I walked under the tall trees with you. I felt sure then that I could face any situation in life with serenity, confidence. I felt I would never lose that inspiration. Today, after battling with lawyers, bill collectors, and sitting for weeks in the witness chair in Superior Court, I feel like a truck had run over me."

"Forget about Eerde, what you felt and thought and did there. When you divide life between the beautiful woods of Eerde and the ugly business world of Los Angeles, you create a hopeless conflict. You long for a memory and fight the reality of your life now."

"You're telling me to fully accept my present situation, without complaining."

"No, to accept is an attitude of the mind. To understand is to see, to perceive at the deepest level, and be free."

"I understand and perceive this, Krishnaji. That I am unhappy, in pain, frustrated. A life without conflict, such as you talk about, seems to me, at this point in my life, totally out of reach."

"It's really easy," he said casually. "But you complicate things. You don't let Life paint the picture. You insist on doing it your own way."

"You're a spiritual genius, Krishnaji. Most of us don't have any particular talent in that respect."

"No, no," he protested. "That's just an excuse for not facing yourself. The very fact that you are here with me now shows you have the potential."

"I thought I did a while back," I said, thinking of the great joyous laughter I had experienced. "It's gone now. That's the sad part of all this. You have moments when you think you've made a breakthrough, then the next day you're in the soup again. Men like Walt Whitman and Edward Carpenter spoke about moments of great illumination, but they lost it, all but the memory of it."

"They tried to hang on to it," said Krishnaji, as if he were well acquainted with the lives of these great mystics. "They didn't let it come to them."

"Are you in constant touch with the reality you call Liberation?"

"There's no separation," he said. Then, after a moment: "I am an example. I have cleaned the slate. Life paints the picture."

There was a long silence. The fire crackled in the fireplace; the wind whistled in the orange grove. Then Krishnaji spoke about a subject we had often discussed before: the importance of being a spiritual aristocrat, which he obviously was to his fingertips, of totally rejecting the deadening mediocrity which engulfed the world, of abandoning oneself to that great spiritual adventure which is unique to every person.

"You have had great teachers," I said. "You have reportedly taken several initiations and have been especially trained and guided for your role as World Teacher. Is it reasonable to expect that we who have not had any of these advantages can attain what you have discovered?"

"I took the long road to find the simple Union. And because of that, because I have attained, you too can find the simple Union."

I had quickly scribbled some notes, which Krishnaji thought useless. We talked some more and then Krishnaji picked up his big Mexican hat and sauntered out, advising me to go to bed early, that I needed the rest. But that would prove a difficult task. I went over my notes and expanded them, then glanced at some of the interesting books* on the living room shelves. My mind was racing; there was no possibility of sleep. I went out for a walk, but quickly returned because of the evening chill. Arya Vihara is a spooky place at night. I had been told that Dr. Besant had magnetically sealed off the place to keep "uninvited astral entities" from loitering on the premises. But the fact was that the night noises here were scary. No doubt they were caused by the expanding of the wood in the daytime with the heat, and the contracting of it with the evening chill. The effect, however, was disturbing. On top of it was the great force generated by Krishnaji, which did not leave with him. The house still felt like the central dynamo of a power plant.

I went to bed, closed my eyes and tried to go to sleep. Impossible. The creaking, thumping, bumping noises no longer bothered me. It was that inescapable, pervading, challenging power that filled the house which I seemed unable to adjust to. At about three in the morning, without a wink of sleep, I could no longer cope with what a friend of mine had called "Krishnaji's roaring *kundalini*."** I got dressed and went out for a long walk. The sun was peeking

---

* Krishnamurti was a contemplative mystic, not a studious man of letters. His favorite reading was mystery novels, and he also enjoyed nonfiction books, especially about nature. His "library" was more a collection of books presented to him by some authors he knew and other gifts.

** "According to Yoga philosophy," writes Mary Lutyens in *Krishnamurti: The Years of Awakening*, "certain force centers in the human body are awakened at

over Topa Topa when I returned. I had walked miles, but I was so filled with the restless energy I had "caught" at Arya Vihara that I felt I could have walked back to Hollywood.

At breakfast that morning Krishnaji asked me if I had had a good, restful night. When I told him what had happened, he laughed. I said, "I thought if I didn't get out quick and walk fast I'd go out of my mind, like Fenn Germer." Fenn Germer was a young devotee of Krishnaji's who had worked for him at Arya Vihara and Eerde, and who had to be taken to a mental institution after suffering a nervous breakdown.

"The trouble with Fenn was that he had completely repressed sex. I don't think that will ever be the case with you, Sidney," he laughed.

I stayed on several more days at Arya Vihara, enjoying Krishnaji's companionship, the unique beauty of the valley and the fine weather. They were restful, happy days. Either I had become adjusted to Krishnaji's "roaring kundalini" or else he, compassionately, had turned it off for my benefit. There were no more serious discussions. I helped him clean the stable, which a sloppy cow kept messing up, helped with the dishes, took long walks with him, talked about unimportant things, laughed and read the "nut" mail. Krishnaji's "fan" mail, which was voluminous, was answered by his secretary in Hollywood. But the "nut" mail he kept aside and showed me for my edification. One hilarious letter was written only along the margins of the paper. It stated that both the writer and Krishnaji

---

various stages of evolution. The kundalini, sometimes called the Serpent Fire, is the force center at the base of the spine. Right living, high thinking and unselfish activity are said to be essential conditions for the awakening of kundalini, which is part of the practice of true Yoga. The awakening brings with it a tremendous release of energy and the power to see clairvoyantly."

were "electrical eggs" specially hatched in order to save a crazy world. There were suggestions on how the world's redemption might be accomplished, including instructions on how to prepare certain foods, and when to eat them, in order to attain enlightenment. This letter should have been preserved; only a totally scrambled brain could have written it.

In the car, just before leaving, thinking about the inner treasure I had discovered at Eerde, but had not found again at Arya Vihara, I said, "I want to rediscover something that I first experienced at Eerde." Krishnaji was silent for a long moment, during which I thought, uneasily, that he might ask me what it was I had experienced. He didn't. He said simply, "Go ahead, do it."

About this time a big event occurred at Arya Vihara: Rosalind and Rajagopal became the proud parents of a baby girl, Radha. The new arrival became the center of attraction. Krishnaji was completely upstaged by the baby, and he seemed to enjoy it. He became very fond of Radha, picking her up at every opportunity and planting a kiss on her baby cheek. It was fun watching Krishnaji in his new role of "loving uncle." Radha would grow into a lovely child who fully returned Krishnaji's love. She called him Krinch.

7

KRISHNAJI RETURNED TO EUROPE AND INDIA. MY RESPON-
sibilities at home as unwilling head of the family had in-
creased when my brother, John, went off to rediscover his
roots in Costa Rica. I kept thinking about the "miracle at
Eerde," wondering dejectedly, as I had before, whether it
would become just a memory for the rest of my life. But
Krishnaji's indirect exhortation at Arya Vihara to "go
ahead, do it!" jabbed at me.

The Hollywood hills, just a few blocks north of my

home, were still undeveloped. There were only dirt roads leading to them, and narrow, untrodden paths in the hills themselves, leading nowhere. The hills were unspoiled and untrammeled, full of singing birds and small wildlife. I would walk up there and sit silently by the hour, not trying to entice the sought-after experience, for I knew this method didn't work, but simply trying to quiet my restless mind and emotions and learn to be at peace with myself. My senses became more acute. I heard bird melodies I had never been aware of and saw curious little creatures staring at me that I had never before noticed. Many days passed, but the Presence I sought remained a distant stranger.

One afternoon I caught sight of a hawk way up high, stalking some earthbound creature. Its flight was a thing of sheer beauty. I recalled how, as a boy on our coffee plantation in Costa Rica, I used to lie on my back for the longest time watching these superb fliers overhead circle leisurely, then suddenly sweep down to catch their unsuspecting prey. I thought, anyone who could ever fly like that would need nothing else in life. I was absorbed in watching this perfect flier when all at once the wondrous joy seized my heart. It had returned! I was ecstatic. I let it carry me higher and higher, in rhythmic waves of joy. But the "altitude" and intensity of it held me back somewhat. I knew I was dealing with a tremendous force entirely new in my life, and although I realized I must eventually let go completely, something kept me from surrendering completely to it. At Eerde, even though I never spoke to Krishnaji about it, for reasons I have already stated, there was always the comforting thought that I could go to him if I felt incapable of handling the situation myself. Here I was all alone in the untrammeled brush of the Hollywood hills, among wild rabbits, gophers and raccoons. What if I momentarily passed out?

Sometimes I felt that could really happen, the experience was so potent. My feeling was that I should proceed cautiously, stay "in control" (a terrible concept instilled in me from childhood) before allowing myself to be inexorably swept to unknown depths. But I promised myself to go a little further and deeper every day. Nothing else mattered.

From that day on I arranged my workaday life so that I would be free by three or four in the afternoon to tramp up Nichols Canyon to my favorite hideaway spot in the hills, there to quietly await the pleasure of the joyous Presence. It came regularly now, sometimes tentatively and timidly, at other times in a kind of stupendous rush, depending on my ability to let go and to maintain a certain quality of passive vitality. It came always in rhythmic waves, each wave stronger than the preceding one, carrying me higher and higher, or perhaps it would be more accurate to say deeper and deeper—a dynamic force that at times felt almost unbearable, as if another wave could shatter something inside. On such occasions I would have to step out of its main path, as it were, no longer remaining completely passive, letting it "unwind" itself to a tempo I could comfortably handle.

One evening, on my way home from the hills, I was so filled with that shining joy that everything my eyes met, whether a human being, an animal, a tree or a rock, called forth an outpouring of love. The earth and the sky seemed to blend exquisitely in a new relationship, and as I walked along the narrow road, my body felt possessed of a vitality, harmony and balance I had never before experienced. My mind was tranquil and crystal-clear. It was a superb "trip." And I knew that it was as natural, genuine and legitimate as the ground under my feet. When I got home, a friend of the family who had come over for dinner exclaimed, upon seeing me, "Look at Sidney! Look at his face. He must be in love!" How right she was. But how difficult it would be to explain that it was not the kind of love she was thinking of.

What has all this to do with Krishnamurti? Everything! Through his extraordinary personality he had opened a door within me that led to a new and exciting dimension. It had closed for a while. Then it had marvelously reopened. What followed, however, was anticlimactic, and difficult to handle, as are all deeply stirring "spiritual" experiences, I believe, when not properly understood and digested. You discover an exciting but unknown inner dimension of endless possibilities. Your safe, familiar world is challenged to its foundation. You stand back to reflect, and before you know it, you have lost the vital thrust that first brought you to the threshold. I think experiences of this nature are one of a kind in a person's life. If you do not seize the moment and go through the magic opening, without reservation or vacillation, it will probably close, leaving at best a tiny aperture to remind you of what might have been. Attitude is all-important. Looking back, I have to admit that my attitude lacked that singleheartedness that is one's only compass in the approach to this uncharted sea. Other paths enticed me, other youthful interests. The Shining Joy is a jealous mistress. It will have all of you or nothing.

When Krishnaji returned from India that year, I called him at Arya Vihara, anxious to see him and hoping that in his unique way he might, perhaps, ignite again the smoldering spark that had given my life spiritual meaning and joy only a year past. He said he was coming to Hollywood the following day and asked me to meet him at the Star Headquarters bungalow on Beachwood Drive, where I had gone previously to hear him talk informally to a group of friends.

82

It was wonderful to see him again. He appeared to be in excellent health and was in great spirits, laughing with that childlike spontaneity that was so delightful and contagious. Whenever I heard a joke or anecdote I thought would tickle him, I'd file it away in my mind to spring on him at our next meeting, just to hear that sunny burst of laughter.

It was a warm afternoon when we sat under the shade of a big lemon tree in the backyard of the bungalow, facing each other. I was in no mood for jokes of any kind this time, and he, sensing my state of mind, was serious and pensive. He asked me what was bothering me. All the unhappiness and frustrations of the past months suddenly welled up in me. I swallowed hard. I felt that if I said anything there would be tears in my eyes, so for a long time I sat silently before him. Finally, I blurted out something about the harshness and dishonesty of the business world I had been plunged into after my father's death, without mentioning what was really eating me up: the self-exile from that special and enchanted world he had opened up in me only a year ago. I thought I knew what his answer would be—that that world was here and now, within me, that I had covered it up by my own stupidity and would have to uncover it again by myself if I wanted it. Words, words, I thought. I wanted to tap that deep well again by the same sort of magical means by which I had first experienced it—sweetly, effortlessly, unbidden. So the all-important subject remained silent and unexpressed. Just the same, I had a feeling he knew well what was gnawing at me.

After another long silence, he asked about the state of my finances. I told him I was flat broke, to add to my other troubles. He called Rajagopal, who was inside in his office, and told him to write out a check in my favor for five hundred dollars. I was embarrassed and mortified, as I had never intended for him to dip into his own inadequate funds to help me out. Rajagopal was confused and hesitant. By the look on his face he must have thought this was some kind of joke. Krishnaji, however, gave the order again, in a voice that left no doubt he meant it. Rajagopal went back inside. Although I was immensely grateful for Krishnaji's generous offer, I felt I should not accept the loan, because I knew he needed the money himself. But he brushed aside all my objections and insisted I take the money. When Rajagopal returned with the check, I said I would have to have some time to pay it back. Krishnaji told me to take all the time I needed. Taking the check from Rajagopal's hand, he gave it to me. With the check in my pocket, I took both his hands in mine—and the tears I had managed to repress all afternoon found their way out.

The following week Krishnaji left for Europe. Two weeks later Rajagopal was on the phone, demanding repayment of the loan right away. I reminded him that Krishnaji had said I could take my time repaying it. He responded that Krishnaji knew nothing about business and that he was there to see that no one took advantage of him! A powerful flash of anger shot through me, but before I could say anything he was sending greetings to the family. Then he hung up. I decided to borrow the money somewhere and pay him back immediately. Tom, the vegetable man, who used to drive his old truck, laden with home-grown produce, from his little farm in the San Fernando Valley into Hollywood, came to my rescue. The loan was immediately paid off.

Krishnaji's tour of South America was in the planning stage the following year when he returned to Ojai. He and I had talked about it often, and it was understood I would be going along as a sort of liaison between him and the press. It was a logical choice, and no one had questioned it. I was Krishnaji's close friend, was acquainted with his teaching and spoke Spanish fluently. But I had not figured on the great influence Rajagopal exercised on Krishnaji's mundane affairs. He was running the tour, and he decided that Byron Casselberry, who had been taking Spanish lessons, should go instead. I was greatly disappointed, but not too much surprised. I knew I was not Rajagopal's boy, never had been.

The tour was a great disappointment to Krishnaji. Although he talked in Chile, Uruguay, Brazil and Argentina, he felt that insufficient preparation had been made for his talks in these countries and that to give two or three lectures in each city he visited was simply not enough to get his teaching across. The Central American and West Indies tour was canceled altogether. On July 3, 1935, Krishnaji wrote to my sister, Mrs. Edith Field Povedano, who was the Costa Rican representative for the Star Publishing Trust, and in charge of the proposed tour:

Dear Mrs. Povedano:

I know many of you will have been preparing and looking forward to our visit. Some of you, I am sure, must have made many sacrifices to have us visit your country. Knowing all this, and knowing what a keen disappointment it will be to you, I have decided after great consideration not to visit the countries of Central America and the West Indies (Cuba, Dominican Republic and Puerto Rico) during this tour. Please do not think that this is some passing fancy or a decision of fatigue; but after very careful deliberation, I have come to this conclusion. I know many of you will be very disappointed, but if I may ask you, please try to understand the reason for this sudden change and postponement.

This short South American visit has again convinced
me that it is utterly futile to give only one or two lectures
in each place; and I find that though I have stayed in
some countries several weeks, there is very little com-
prehension of what I am saying. So I feel very strongly
that it would be a waste of your money and my energy to
visit your country merely for a week or two. Even
though there may be keen disappointment, I am sure
you will appreciate why I have come to this decision . . .
Of course, this does not mean that I am not coming to
your country in the future . . .

If I may suggest, before I visit your country, there
should be a thorough preparation through the distribution of the reports of my recent talks so that, when I
come, what I say will not be entirely new and puzzling
to the audience.

Such preparation through the distribution of
Krishnaji's translated talks is exactly what had been going
on in Costa Rica for two years previously. One of his translated talks appeared every Sunday in the literary supple-
ment of *La Tribuna*, then Costa Rica's leading newspaper.
Every shipment of his books was quickly sold out, and
there was a large discussion group in San José, the country's capital, which included many professionals, intellectuals, artists. Nowhere else in Latin America had his
teachings had greater exposure. A committee of hard-
working, devoted friends had been laboring for many
months to ensure that his words would reach as many
people as possible. They felt that the unusual situation in
Costa Rica fully justified Krishnaji's visit there, and I entirely agreed with them. Their bitter disappointment at the
cancellation of the tour was understandable. In their opinion, Krishnaji had been very badly advised.

Krishnaji's ship was due to stop at Puntarenas, on

Costa Rica's Pacific coast, on its way to the States. A large delegation made the eighty-mile train trip from San José to meet him at the port. This, at least, would not be taken from them. My brother, John, was among them, as well as my sister Edith, who had been the national organizer of the Order of the Star in the East in Costa Rica for years before its dissolution. Krishnaji had announced beforehand that he would give no interviews on board ship, but a young cub reporter had hopefully gone along with the rest when he was told by his boss that if he didn't get his interview he'd be out of a job. John waited until the other visitors had disembarked and Krishnaji had taken his afternoon nap. Then he cornered him and told him about the reporter's dilemma. Krishnaji immediately granted the interview, inviting my brother and the reporter to the ship's bar for a cool beer. Abstemious all his life, he, of course, did not touch it.

The annual spring talks and discussions at the Oak Grove had been going on for many years when I realized with a shock that the excitement and passion for self-discovery no longer played an important part in my life. I felt I had gone stale, had reached a saturation point at the verbal and intellectual level of Krishnaji's teaching, and needed a respite from it all for a while. So I would drive the family to the Oak Grove and then quietly disappear into the hills beyond until it was all over (though I could still hear the distant echo of Krishnaji's voice). Then I would walk down to pick them up at a predestined place. On one of these occasions I ran into Krishnaji, who was leaving the Oak Grove with a group of friends. One of them, a woman I knew, said to me, "Wasn't it a wonderful talk?"

"I don't know," I said. "I didn't hear it."

I answered her startled look by turning to Krishnaji.

"I'm going through a stage, Krishnaji, where I simply cannot hear another talk."

Krishnaji laughed. "Thank God for that," he shot back.

Before leaving for Europe that year, Krishnaji asked me over for lunch at Arya Vihara. After his afternoon siesta he, Rajagopal and I drove over to Matilija Hot Springs in the northern part of the valley, as Rajagopal wanted to try the hot sulphur baths for his arthritis.

We slid into three separate tubs, separated by thin partitions into small cubicles and filled with hot, strong-smelling sulphur water. Beside each tub was a small table with a large glass full of the pungent water. It was supposed to be good for you, very cleansing, the management told us. I picked up the glass and smelled the stuff. Instantly I decided I would rather be unclean, and put it back on the table. Rajagopal had a similar reaction. But Krishnaji, always intent on discovering something new, took a big gulp. Somnolently relaxed and partly overcome by the sulphur fumes, I was suddenly startled by a thunderous belch in Krishnaji's cubicle. "Are you all right, Krishnaji?" I called.

"I just swallowed some of this foul water," came his voice.

We all had a big laugh over this incident afterward, but we decided to keep it to ourselves because stories like this have a way of growing in substance and detail to unrecognizable proportions. Krishnaji, however, had to repeat the story several times that afternoon because of his sulphuric breath.

8

THE SUBJECT OF EDUCATION, ALWAYS CLOSE TO KRISHNAJI'S heart, was a matter of lively discussion at Arya Vihara years before the Happy Valley School came into being after the Second World War. Rosalind had gathered a small group of students at the primary level whose parents shared Krishnaji's views on education and considered it a privilege to have their children attend school under Krishnaji's roof. Even though he lived with them only three or four months during the year, his presence was pervasive, and he seemed to invade the soul of the small group, giving them moral and spiritual guidance without imposing strict rules and regulations. Rosalind's daughter, Radha, her nephew, David Weidemann, and a charming Southern boy, Jimmy Schloss, who, years later, became Radha's husband, formed the nucleus of a growing student body. Krishnaji had a special knack for relating to each one of the preadolescent students in a relaxed, give-and-take spirit which revealed itself in a warm camaraderie between them and him. He played games with the students, helped them with their homework, went out walking with them.

I remember how, one time when Krishnaji was ill and confined to his room, they all were so concerned about him that they observed strict silence during his resting periods and always were eager to be given the chance to take his food into his bedroom. I got to know them all well, for Rosalind would often ask me to meet one of the new arrivals at the Los Angeles airport and drive him over to Arya Vihara.

As the group grew into adolescence, the educating process grew more complex and demanding. It was at this point that it was decided to start a regular school, the Happy Valley School, with Krishnaji and his teaching as its guiding light. Land was purchased*; buildings were erected; teachers were hired. Guido Ferrando, a distin-

---

* Krishnamurti was still with the Theosophists when Annie Besant launched a fund-raising appeal to establish a school that would embody the work of the World Teacher. Two parcels of land were purchased. One consisted of 240 acres in the western, or lower, part of the Ojai Valley, where the summer camp and later talks took place in the Oak Grove. Another 450 acres were bought even earlier in the eastern part of the valley, near Arya Vihara, but it took two decades before the Happy Valley School was started there in 1946. Aldous Huxley, among others, was closely associated with the Happy Valley School, which served as a prototype for other schools Krishnamurti later established in India and England.

guished educator, was appointed director, and for a while, under his wise and sensitive direction, the school thrived. But this early success didn't last long. Ferrando either stepped out or was forced out, and eventually Krishnaji himself was pushed aside. He later said, "The school slipped through our fingers." Rosalind Rajagopal took over as director.

The school came inevitably to reflect the personality of its new head. A good fund-raiser and efficient administrator, Rosalind was totally lacking in the one essential quality of a true educator—the ability to reach out beyond the classroom and touch a student's heart.*

With its auspicious beginning, it is not surprising that the school was carried on by its own momentum to rise for a while above the average educational institution. Eventually, however, the unique quality of experimentation with new values and educational approaches brought over by the promising seedling from Arya Vihara gave way to old and crystallized establishment attitudes and values, implemented by a staff which, except for two or three of its members, were mediocre if not incompetent.

Krishnaji was in Ojai when war broke out in Europe in September 1939. In the preceding months he had expressed his strongly anti-war views before large and sympathetic audiences at his Oak Grove talks. But with the end of the "phoney war," the invasion of Flanders and the fall of France, England, under siege, remained alone to fight Hitler. Although not yet formally at war, the United States was rapidly becoming, to all intents and purposes, a bellig-

---

* After the rift with Rajagopal, which left the management of the Happy Valley School with Rosalind, Krishnamurti wanted his educational philosophy kept alive in Ojai. He established the still thriving Oak Grove School in 1975 at the western end of the valley, where the Krishnamurti Foundation owns land.

erent. Under the Lend-Lease program, a flotilla of Liberty ships plied the Atlantic Ocean under U.S. naval escort to keep England's imperiled lifeline intact. Criticism of the war and dissent were virtually stifled. Everyone was jittery. As a scion of a prominent expatriate family, I had an appointment as Costa Rican consul in Los Angeles at this time, and I knew that the FBI was on the hunt for "subversives"—that is, anyone who expressed views in opposition to the coming bloodbath.

It was under this cloud of war hysteria that Krishnaji opened his series of Oak Grove talks in Ojai late in May, 1941. I was concerned for him and wondered whether under the unusual circumstances he would soften his anti-war remarks. He did not. He expressed his views as clearly and bluntly as if the war did not exist, lashing out at "this mass murder called war," and proclaiming, "To kill another is the greatest evil." He disarmed hostile questioners with a quiet, even gentle, reminder that their problem was not with the person who disagreed with them but with their own innate hostility. "The war within you," he kept saying, "is the war you should be concerned about, not the war outside." Many people left in a huff, flinging harsh and sometimes insulting words at him as they walked out. Others in the audience retaliated in his favor, in equally strong terms. At one point I fully expected a brawl to break out. Krishnaji remained calm and collected through it all, waiting calmly until the disturbance subsided.

Standing under one of the leafy oaks, I could not help but admire his "cool" under these trying circumstances, and I wondered if he would be allowed by the officials keeping an eye on him to finish his talks. Men from the FBI, one of whom I knew, were in the audience. I was sure they were not happy about what they were hearing.

Without pulling his punches in any way, Krishnaji went through the scheduled series of talks in the Oak Grove without any untoward incidents until July 14, the occasion of the last public lecture he was to give in this country, or any other country, for the duration of the war. After years of continuous traveling and lecturing, he was very tired, and thought this was the appropriate time to take a long rest.

This period thus marked his longest continuous stay at Arya Vihara, although he made visits to various friends both out of the state and in California, including several trips to the Monterey Peninsula to visit his friend Robinson Jeffers, the great Carmel poet. After reading Jeffers' epic poem "Dear Judas," I raved to Krishnaji about it. Jeffers had painted a picture of Jesus so moving, so human and compassionate, that it almost made a Christian out of me. Krishnaji promised to read it. Knowing that Jeffers was a recluse and a very private man, I asked Krishnaji, after one of his visits to him, what they had done and what they had talked about. Krishnaji answered, "We went for a long walk through the woods and never said a word."

One day the phone rang. It was Krishnaji, calling from Ojai. He wanted to know whether we could put up Koos Van der Leeuw, who had arrived unexpectedly at a time when they were all filled up at Arya Vihara. I said that we would be very happy to put him up, but that he would probably sleep somewhat uncomfortably, as we didn't have a bed long enough for him. Krishnaji laughed and said Koos wouldn't mind: "He's used to it."

The following day the tall, bald-headed Dutch philosopher arrived at our home in Hollywood, wearing a boy scout's outfit—khaki shirt and abbreviated shorts—that made him appear endlessly tall. I apologized for the size of the bed. Good-naturedly he said it was warm weather and he didn't mind sleeping with his toes sticking out of the bed. The following day I drove him to Santa Barbara, where he stayed for a few weeks. He wanted to be close to Ojai in order to see Krishnaji. I don't know whether he rebuked him for that toothpaste joke at Eerde. The fact is he couldn't forget it; nor did he see anything funny about it. "Krishnaji will be a great teacher when he matures," he said to me on our way to Santa Barbara.

Some weeks later Koos was back in Hollywood. He wanted to buy an airplane which he would pilot on a lecture tour of Africa he was planning. I took him to Lockheed Aircraft, whose president, Robert Gross, was a friend of mine. Koos chose a sleek, twin-motor model and gave Gross a check for eighty thousand dollars. The plane was flown to Holland, where Koos took possession of it. He embarked upon his African lecture tour as planned. On his way back home, he crashed in Kenya and was killed.*

Late in 1941 Krishnaji faced the problem of getting an extension to his permission to stay in this country. Normally, this would have been an easy matter. He had been getting extensions previously without any difficulty. But now certain elements in the Immigration Department were opposed to it, no doubt influenced by critical reports from FBI men who had stood watchfully under the oak trees the previous year, listening to Krishnaji propound his anti-war views. Krishnaji and I talked about the matter over the phone. Friends of his in Washington, D.C., were pressuring the immigration officials to grant the extension, but they

---

* Ruth and John Tettemer's daughter, Eve, says that this episode happened well before the war. She remembers as a small child in California when news came that Koos (who was her godfather) had crashed during a solo flight over the African continent. The body and the wreckage were never found, and many people assumed that this interesting man, who had undergone personal analysis with Freud, had committed suicide.

were stalling. Finally they said they wanted certain affidavits signed by people who had some standing in the community. Personally, I rated my own standing in the community at zero, but it was a fact that I was consul of Costa Rica at Los Angeles, with jurisdiction over five western states, an important position in a war-torn world, and many people are impressed by labels. Krishnaji thought that my signing the affidavits would help, and, of course, I was happy to oblige him. His formal request came by letter:

November 13, 1941.

Dear Sidney:

As my permission to stay in this country expires on February 7, 1942, it has been suggested that I collect some affidavits to be sent to the Immigration Authorities; so I hope you do not mind my writing to you to ask if you would kindly sign the enclosed affidavits; but if for any reason whatsoever, you feel in any way inclined not to, I shall understand.

These affidavits have to be sent to the Immigration Authorities, and they require that the status of each person be fully explained. By "status" they mean occupation or profession and their general standing.

I am very sorry that I have to trouble you to write about yourself, but apparently this is what the Immigration Authorities require to make the affidavits worth while, and I sincerely hope that you don't mind.

If I may ask you, would you please send *all the three* copies of the affidavit, filled out and signed, back to me in the enclosed envelope as soon as possible.

I am really very sorry to bother you with all this, but I hope you will understand my writing to you.

Sister Erma kindly said that she will notarize the affidavits.

With love,

Yours,

Krishnamurti .

Krishnamurti

The official documents were so cold and impersonal, however, and the stakes so high, that I decided to write directly to the immigration authorities. I felt extremely awkward writing a "recommendation" for Krishnaji. It was ridiculous and entirely ironic, but somehow in line with a topsy-turvy world. Krishnaji, at any rate, was pleased about my letter, so I sent it along. It read as follows:

Nov. 18, 1941.

To the Immigration Authorities:

It has been my good fortune, and that of my family's, to have known Mr. J. Krishnamurti for over 15 years, during which time we have listened with the greatest interest to a great many of his lectures and informal talks.

My father, the late Walter J. Field, a native of Montpelier, Vermont, and a recognized authority in international banking and finance, having been prominent in this city for many years as a member of the Regional Board of Directors of the Bank of America, and founder and President of the Field Building and Loan Assn., helped to build a center in Ojai, Calif., where Mr. Krishnamurti has lectured practically every year since 1928. My father considered that the establishment of this center afforded a splendid opportunity to the great number of people in California interested in Mr. Krishnamurti's ideas to come directly in contact with his teachings.

My family and myself, who have lived in Hollywood for over twenty years, have attended Mr. Krishnamurti's outdoor talks in the Ojai Valley since their inception over 13 years ago, and have always felt that Southern California was indeed fortunate in having a place where a man of the moral and spiritual stature of Mr. Krishnamurti could come and express his ideas.

Yours very truly,
Sidney T. Field
Consul of Costa Rica.

The extension was granted. Thus, Krishnamurti's stay in Ojai for the duration of the war was assured.

The frequency of my trips to Arya Vihara decreased during the war years. Work at the consulate, plus writing assignments on the side, kept me very busy, and gas rationing sharply curtailed driving, even though I was able to get an extra share of gas coupons because of my diplomatic status.

There were, nevertheless, periodic visits to Arya Vihara, and interesting lunch sessions. It was at one of these luncheons that I first met Aldous Huxley and his first wife, Maria, who had become close friends of Krishnaji's and the Rajagopals'. Huxley was a fascinating personality, one of the most brilliant thinkers of his time, and a walking encyclopedia. He admired and respected Krishnaji as a great spiritual teacher, but he didn't hesitate in taking him to task when he disagreed with him. Their philosophical and metaphysical discussions were particularly lively. Krishnaji would often make a general, sweeping statement, as he was wont to do, minimizing the significance of the intellect in resolving the enormous problems of life. Huxley would then launch a rebuttal, very quietly, with always the right word at his command, spoken in the most correct British manner. He would summon all kinds of scientific and historical evidence to indicate the great role intellect had always played in dissipating some of the darkest clouds of ignorance and superstition. It is a pity, indeed, that these fascinating luncheon sessions were not recorded, for these two extraordinary minds, looking at life from their highly individual viewpoints, often produced verbal fireworks.

There were always interesting people visiting Krishnaji at Arya Vihara during his long wartime residence there. Among them was the Viennese actress, Luise Rainer, who admired Krishnaji and thought that with his extraordinary looks and personality he would make a sensational actor, but who never professed any particular interest in his ideas. Her special interest at Arya Vihara was Rosalind, with whom she had developed a close friendship. Although not beautiful by Hollywood standards, she had warmth and vivacity, and a shrewd instinct about advancing her career. Her friendship with me, inevitably gossiped about in Hollywood, had a very practical and unromantic aspect to it: gasoline! Because of my consular position, I had more gas coupons than she did, and could drive her to Arya Vihara when she had used up her allotment. Conversely, when I had exhausted my own supply and felt a need to drive to Ojai to see Krishnaji, I would persuade her to buy black market coupons at inflated prices from a source who would trade only through members of the consular corps. It was a fair deal, I thought. She had the money, and I had the connections.

Toward the end of the war, my trips to Ojai became more frequent again, although not always motivated by a desire to see Krishnaji. I had met and later married a young English actress, Daphne Moore, who had recently come to Ojai from Connecticut with seven former members of Michael Chekhov's studio and touring company. Together they started the High Valley Theater of Ojai, under the direction of Alan Harkness.

When I told Krishnaji that I had married, he seemed quite surprised, which was hardly a shock, considering that he never had a high opinion of marriage.* Nevertheless, he wished me luck. The consensus of opinion at Arya

---

* The Theosophists disapproved of marriage, especially for the higher Initiates, and many marriages were ruined when one of the parties decided to abstain from sex. Krishnamurti wrote to Lady Emily Lutyens (in 1920): "Of course I shall never marry, that is not for me in this life, I have something better to do." In later life Krishnamurti often saw marriage as the domination and oppression of one party by the other, and as a hindrance to attaining liberation from emotional ties.

Vihara was that it wouldn't work out. It didn't. But I was determined to prove them wrong. When I was made to step down from the position of Costa Rican consul due to a change of government in that country, I took a job as a writer at the Walt Disney Studios. I found myself commuting back and forth between the studios and my wife in Ojai while I looked for a place in Ojai that I could afford. It was an exhausting way of life. In the end, the popular consensus was vindicated: it didn't work out.

Krishnaji attended some of the performances of the theater company in Upper Ojai. He particularly liked the eccentric, unconventional Iris Tree, an actress and writer with the group. She was the daughter of Sir Herbert Beerbohm-Tree, the great English theater manager, and knew many people in show business. Her modest Ojai ranch house, a short walk from Arya Vihara, became a mecca for visiting Hollywood celebrities: Charlie Chaplin, Greta Garbo, Yul Brynner, Angela Lansbury, John Huston and many others. They all professed to be greatly interested in Krishnaji's ideas, but I always felt they sensed a threat to their egos in his teaching,* for they stayed safely away from him.

An exception was Rouben Mamoulian, who had directed several of Garbo's pictures. I had known him in Hollywood, and he asked me if I could arrange an interview with Krishnaji. I did. We sat on the lawn behind Arya Vihara—Krishnaji, Mamoulian, Rosalind and I. Mamoulian told us he had just read a book about the Civil War and immediately launched upon his favorite subject: violence is sometimes justified.

---

* Krishnamurti held, with the main body of Eastern philosophies, that the ego stood in the way of spiritual development. He rarely used the personal pronoun and usually referred to himself in the third person, or simply as "K."

"You don't believe in slavery, do you?" he asked Krishnaji.

"No, I don't."

"Would you have taken up arms if that were the only way to free the American slaves, or would you have refused to do anything violent and thus aided the cause of slavery?"

"I cannot answer a hypothetical, abstract question with a positive statement," answered Krishnaji. "The answer to any question relative to conduct must come out of the living moment to which the question is related. Otherwise it's purely an intellectual game."

The discussion went on for some time, with Mamoulian continuing to play the "intellectual game" and Krishnaji sticking to his viewpoint. All the while Mamoulian smoked a large, smelly cigar, thoroughly polluting the atmosphere, apparently unconcerned about how anybody else felt about it. Krishnaji, always the perfect host, suffered through it all uncomplainingly.

Some years later, the film director asked me what would be a good book of Krishnaji's to read. I sent him *Freedom from the Known*. I never heard from him again. When, later in life, I began working with juvenile offenders through the Southern California Counseling Center, I gave the same book to one of my young charges, who was beginning to inquire about moral values. A few days later the boy wrote to me from his place of confinement, summing up his reaction to the book in a single word: "I started to read *Freedom from the Known*. WOW!"

It is not difficult to understand why Krishnaji went out of his way to reach the younger generation.

Dr. Annie Besant and K. in the
late 1920's.

Dr. Annie Besant and K. shortly
before her death.

A more carefree Sidney in Ojai in his twenties.

Sidney.

Sidney visiting back in Costa Rica.

Group picture of leading Theosophists gathered at Camp Ommen. K. is in the middle of the second row. Sidney is fifth from right in the back row, Ruth Roberts is fifth from the left, standing next to the bearded George Arundale, one of the self-styled "apostles." Seventh from the left is Rajagopal, directly behind Rosalind. Next to her, the two tall figures are probably Byron Casselberry and J.J. Van Der Leeuw (Koos).

Ruth Roberts Tettemer.

Ruth Roberts Tettemer and
Sidney.

Sidney in his thirties.

Sidney in his fifties.

Camp Ommen in Holland, where K. announced his resignation as the Theosophists' World Teacher.

Castle Eerde in Holland.

K. with Baron Philip Van Pallandt who donated him Castle Eerde.

The Reluctant Messiah.

9

AFTER THE WAR, KRISHNAJI RESUMED HIS INTERNATIONAL travels and teaching. He spent a great deal more time in India in the tumultuous years before and after independence. Following Mahatma Gandhi's assassination in January 1948, it was to Krishnamurti that Prime Minister Jawaharlal Nehru was said to have turned for strength and consolation. During the 1950s, Krishnaji extended his teaching by establishing schools and by writing books, which would eventually number more than twenty volumes.

Krishnaji's relationship with the efficient but domineering Rajagopal, who had managed his business affairs for thirty-five years, reached a point of rupture in 1960. This unfortunate controversy had been brewing for some time, much to Krishnaji's discomfort and despite his genuine and repeated efforts to settle the matter amicably. The struggle for control over the copyrights to Krishnamurti's writings and over his real estate holdings split the community of his friends into camps.

In autumn 1966, when Krishnaji came to Ojai for the talks at the Oak Grove, he stayed in his cottage at Arya Vihara. I attempted to call him there to make an appointment to see him. The phone was answered by Alain Naude, who had become his secretary after Rajagopal's departure. I explained that I was an old friend of Krishnaji's and wanted to see him. He would not call Krishnaji to the phone, and his manner was guarded and abrupt. I gave him my phone number and asked him to please have Krishnaji call me at his convenience. I didn't hear from either of them, so I thought I would just wait and see Krishnaji after one of the Oak Grove talks. This, however, wasn't easy that year. An unusually large number of people crowded in on him after his talks. He appeared uncomfortable with them and quickly got away and into his car. Once I saw him as he was being driven away from the Oak Grove. We waved at each other, and I thought, well, this is it for this year.

Following the last talk, however, Krishnaji ran into my brother, John, and asked him to tell me to come and see him at Arya Vihara on a certain afternoon. Promptly at two o'clock on the appointed day, I drove into Arya Vihara. There were eight or ten old friends of Krishnaji in the living room. Alain Naude came in to announce that he would be in presently. The secretary was followed by Mrs. Mary

Zimbalist, Krishnaji's closest companion during the last twenty-five years of his life, who charmed everyone present. After a long wait, Krishnaji showed up. He appeared uncomfortable and ill at ease, a feeling that persisted throughout the visit. I had never seen him in this mood. There was very little of the warmth and vibrancy one had always associated with him; he was distant and uncommunicative. After about a half hour of social chitchat, he got up and bade us farewell. I drove home that afternoon with a sense of sadness. Krishnaji's manner, and the expression on his face, showed clearly that his stay at Arya Vihara that year had been a great trial to him.

A few days after our visit, Krishnaji left for New York. He did not return to his old home in Ojai until after the 1974 court settlement with Rajagopal, when the property was returned to him via the Krishnamurti Foundation.

The years leading up to that settlement were trying for all concerned. During the summer of 1969, Krishnaji published a statement regarding his break with Rajagopal in the *Bulletin*, the official organ of the Krishnamurti Foundation of America:

STATEMENT FROM KRISHNAMURTI

Many people have written expressing concern over Krishnamurti's disassociation from Krishnamurti Writings Inc., (KWINC.) and are asking why this has happened. Krishnamurti feels that the public should be informed, because they have for the past forty years supported his work and made substantial contributions to Krishnamurti Writings Inc., on his account.

For the past ten years Krishnamurti has repeatedly asked Mr. Rajagopal, the President of Krishnamurti Writings Inc., to inform and consult him about its policy and affairs. Mr. Rajagopal has consistently refused to do

so and denied Krishnamurti access to his own manuscripts and archives in Krishnamurti Writings. In addition Krishnamurti recently learned that through the
years changes were made in Krishnamurti Writings Inc.
excluding him from all say in its affairs. Krishnamurti
tried many times to settle matters amicably with Mr.
Rajagopal and members of the Board of Krishnamurti
Writings Inc., but to no avail.

He very much regrets that it has been necessary to
appeal for funds all over again, but the money given to
Krishnamurti Writings for his work is at present tied up
in that organization and is not at his disposal.

Every precaution has been taken in the formation of
Krishnamurti Foundation of England and the Krishnamurti Foundation of America to insure that a similar
problem will not occur in the future.

Before Krishnaji's return to Ojai, I had occasion to
listen to a tape made by a mutual friend, Albert Blackburn,
in Saanen, Switzerland, in 1968, in which Krishnaji
pleaded with Rajagopal to come to an amicable resolution
of their controversy. Krishnaji's attitude was entirely con-
ciliatory. It was perfectly clear that the whole thing was
extremely distasteful and painful to him, and that although
he was firm in his resolution to break away from Rajagopal
and his control of Krishnamurti Writings, Inc., he was most
anxious to do so without fuss or recourse to legal means.
Knowing some of the factors that prompted the final break, I
thought Krishnaji's patience and friendly attitude toward
Rajagopal were truly remarkable. The latter, however,
would not consent to listen to the tape, although Al Blackburn told me that he had repeatedly asked him to do so.
Even more surprising was the attitude of some of Rajagopal's friends in Ojai, who also stubbornly refused to listen

to this revealing tape, in which Krishnaji presented his case for the first time.

Rajagopal was adamant in his refusal to go along with Krishnaji's demands, and in all fairness it must be said that he had a good basis for his position. He maintained that Krishnaji had given him the copyright to all his properties and hence he was not obligated to answer any questions regarding the controversy. This was true. Krishnaji, totally unconcerned with worldly affairs, had signed a document in 1957 in Poona, India, to this effect:

> I hereby give the proprietorship in all my writings previous to this date as well as from this date forward to Krishnamurti Writings, Inc., Ojai, California, U.S.A.; London, England; and Madras, India.

> Further, I authorize Mr. D. Rajagopal, President of Krishnamurti Writings, Inc. to make any arrangement that may be necessary with regard to the publication of all books and articles that I have written or may write. He has my full authorization to make contracts or agreements on my behalf or to authorize contracts to be made on my behalf in connection with the publication of my writings.

> Made in duplicate and good faith.

Later on, Krishnaji realized the mistake he had made and had his lawyer bring up the matter in court. The court declared the copyright agreement with Rajagopal null and void. Rajagopal, however, refused to accept this decision. To add to the tension, Rajagopal also refused to readmit Krishnaji as a member of the board of Krishnamurti Writings, Inc., after Krishnaji had previously relinquished this position.

Soon after the tape incident, I received a seven-page

letter from the late James Vigeveno, who lived in Ojai. This gentleman, who had been a very successful art dealer and who had also been devoted to Krishnaji, now came out with an outrageous blast at his former idol. It was sent to everyone on the mailing list of Krishnamurti Writings.

I will quote only certain excerpts from this ugly, abusive and repetitive letter, excerpts which reveal, I think, its overall mentality. A proper response would require a book in itself, together with a full transcript of the litigation that preceded the settlement of the controversy.

Ojai, July 1969

TO FRIENDS OF MINE AND THOSE
WHO HAVE BEEN HURT

Since 1927, now forty-two years ago, when I first met Krishnamurti, I have always been a great admirer and friend, and have ever since then been deeply interested in his teachings. During these years I have worked much for him, have been a trustee and later Vice-President of Krishnamurti Writings, Inc. until the end of 1966 . . . But by 1960 things began to change.

The tension became stronger and stronger, and an open break between Krishnamurti and Rajagopal was proclaimed all over the world. Krishnamurti, who had never wanted anything to do with organizations, now took over personally, with the help of Mr. Naude. He also took over the representatives of the Krishnamurti Writings, Inc. all over the world, and everyone naturally followed the new set-up—a new organization called "The Krishnamurti Foundation." . . .

On October 31st 1968, Krishnaji called me over the telephone and said to me:

"I don't want to talk with Rajagopal alone. I want to meet with the trustees of Krishnamurti Writings, Rajagopal and you. If this does not happen, I am out of it. If we don't meet before November 3rd, the lawyers will take charge. I want at the meeting to be present: Rajago- pal and the trustees, and I will bring: Mrs. Zimbalist, Mr. Naude and Mr. & Mrs. Lilliefelt. But under no cir- cumstances will I see Rajagopal alone.

After this conversation I talked with Rajagopal. Ra- jagopal gave up his insistence to speak with Krishna- murti alone, and agreed to send the following telegram to Krishnamurti on November 2nd, 1968:

"Answering your wish to talk with KWINC. trustees, I can arrange a meeting between you personally and the trustees at the KWINC. office on Besant Road. Please advise date and time you desire after your return from Claremont when more trustees will be available.

"James Vigeveno."

On November 5th I received the following answer:

"I regret very much that Rajagopal and the trustees refused my request for a meeting between *all* of us. I won't come to a meeting alone. The matter is now out of my hands. Krishnamurti." . . .

James Vigeveno

The rest of the letter is given over to a series of absurd, baseless accusations, distortions, half-truths and innu- endos, which have no place in this book.

Having known Krishnamurti since I was a boy, and having been aware of his relationship with Rajagopal and the extraordinary generosity, consideration, loyalty and trust with which he treated him, I was outraged by Vig- eveno's preposterous and insulting manner in defending Rajagopal.

But enough of Vigeveno's outburst. My answer to his

letter was an angry one, but, looking back upon the circumstances, I think it was fully justified.

Aug. 26, 1969

Dear Mr. Vigeveno:
I acknowledge receipt of your TO MY FRIENDS AND THOSE WHO HAVE BEEN HURT. (A stupid appeal to self pity.)

"For the past ten years Krishnamurti has repeatedly asked Mr. Rajagopal, the President of Krishnamurti Writings Inc. to inform and consult him about its policy and affairs. Mr. Rajagopal has consistently refused to do so and denied Krishnamurti access to his own manuscripts and archives in Krishnamurti Writings. In addition Krishnamurti recently learned that through the years changes were made in Krishnamurti Writings Inc. excluding him from all say in its affairs. Krishnamurti tried many times to settle matters amicably with Mr. Rajagopal and members of the Board of Krishnamurti Writings, but to no avail . . . The money given to Krishnamurti Writings for his work is at present tied up in that organization and is not at his disposal."

This, as you're undoubtedly aware, is a quotation from a "Statement from Krishnamurti" published in the Summer issue of the Krishnamurti Foundation Bulletin. It is the crux of the Krishnamurti—Rajagopal controversy.

So, the above being the core of the situation, we have all waited for an official statement from you people. Instead of it we get your "White Paper." In this long-winded document you carefully avoid the central issue and fill up seven long pages with an insulting attack upon the person of Krishnamurti himself.

You state, "One day history will reveal everything." With this statement I'm entirely in agreement. But I'm afraid the verdict of history will be quite different from that which you expect.

Sincerely yours,
Sidney Field

A few days after this letter was mailed, I received a phone call from Rajagopal in Ojai. It appeared that a shocked Vigeveno, who was his neighbor, had rushed over to him with my letter, demanding to know why Rajagopal had ever thought I could be converted to their cause.

Excitedly, Rajagopal started out by telling me that Vigeveno, "this fine, high-minded gentleman" who had always considered himself my friend, was "horribly wounded" by the things I had said, adding that the least I could do under the circumstances was to call him up immediately, or else write him, apologizing. Rajagopal's voice became increasingly wrought up and excited as he appealed to our old friendship and asked me to withhold judgment until he could explain matters. I cut him short and said that if the purpose of his long-distance call was to get me to apologize to Vigeveno, he had wasted his money. "I will never apologize to Vigeveno for a single word in that letter," I said angrily.

"It's all a misunderstanding," said Rajagopal. "I love Krishnaji, and so does James Vigeveno."

"Is that foul letter the way you and Vigeveno express your love for Krishnaji?"

Rajagopal's answer was to ask me to come over to see him, that he would tell me the whole truth, explain everything to me.

"I'll come over tomorrow morning," I said.

"Give me a week's time," Rajagopal responded. "I have to prepare myself."

I shall never forget those words. Why should he need a week's time to explain to an old friend the breakup of his forty-year relationship with Krishnaji? That was the end of our conversation. Then I recalled that Rajagopal had taken a degree in law at Cambridge University. It was obvious to me that in this crisis he had instinctively turned to the old, self-defensive posture of a lawyer in an adversary situation, asking for time to prepare his case before facing the jury—a commendable attitude in a court of law, but a suspect ploy in a private attempt to divulge the "truth" about his relationship with Krishnaji.

Friends who had read my letter to Vigeveno suggested

I send a copy of it to Krishnaji, who was then at Brockwood Park in England, setting up a school and conference center. A couple of weeks later I received Krishnaji's reply:

24th September 1969

My dear Sidney,

Thank you so much for your letter enclosing your reply to Mr. Vigeveno's drivel.

I must say your reply is really very good, and if I may I would like to congratulate you on the way you have gone straight to the point, showing exactly what they are doing.

It is surprising how this letter of Vigeveno's has gone right round the world. They seem to have sent it to India and to many people in Europe, and it seems that they really want to make a scandal out of it all. I am very sorry that all this has come about when everything could have been reasonably, sanely and amicably settled.

I am glad you had a telephone call from Rajagopal and perhaps you may be able to see him and, if possible, help him to get over all this.

I hope you are well, and please give my affection to all the family.

Yours very affectionately,
Krishnamurti

[In K's hand]: Hope to see you next Spring. Hope you are well.

There was also a letter from Mary Zimbalist, who had helped him to set up the Krishnamurti Foundation of America following the schism with Rajagopal:

24th September 1969

Dear Sidney,

If I had a hat I would like to throw it in the air with exuberance at reading your reply to the wretched Vigeveno letter. It has cheered Krishnaji and should be framed in the Archives as a bright blaze of sanity in all this ugly business.

With all warmest wishes,

Yours,
Mary (Zimbalist)

When Krishnaji returned to California the following year, he stayed at the Malibu home of Mrs. Zimbalist, a place of quiet distinction high on a bluff overlooking the sea. I went to see him there. He greeted me affectionately and gave me a beautiful, hand-painted batik silk shawl he had brought from India, a lovely gift that I deeply appreciated.

Mrs. Zimbalist, a gracious hostess, served tea in her elegant living room, which presented a picture view of a becalmed and shimmering Santa Monica Bay. Krishnaji thanked me personally for my letter to Vigeveno, and we talked at length about the unfortunate controversy with Rajagopal. It was difficult for Krishnaji to realize that a man he had regarded as a brother for so many years could turn against him with such fierce hostility. I said that in my opinion this about-face of Rajagopal had been in the making for years, even though apparently he had not noticed it, or thought it unimportant. "I believe that for a long time Rajagopal has harbored a deep resentment against you, Krishnaji."

Krishnaji seemed startled. "But why, why?" he asked.

I said I thought it was the resentment of a vain and ambitious person who hates to play second fiddle to a man of genius. I added that I had wanted to speak to him about the situation on several occasions, but had felt that his loyalty to his "family" would not allow any criticism of it.

Still hoping to resolve the controversy in a friendly way, Krishnaji asked me what I thought should be done. I said that in my opinion he would ultimately have to sue Rajagopal and Krishnamurti Writings, Inc., to settle matters. I offered to consult my lawyer, Robert Kenny, who had been California's attorney general and was at this time a judge of the Superior Court in Los Angeles. Krishnaji thought this was a fine idea, and we agreed that I should make an appointment with Judge Kenny and get back to him.

The following day I called Judge Kenny's office, which had been left in the charge of his associate, Robert Morris, an old and trusted friend. I made an appointment to see Morris about the Krishnamurti matter. A few days later, accompanied by Mrs. Erna Lilliefelt, a trustee of the Krishnamurti Foundation of America who had conducted a thorough investigation of the legal aspects of the controversy, I paid a visit to Morris's office in downtown Los Angeles. We sat around a long conference table, and Mrs. Lilliefelt handed Morris a letter from Krishnaji explaining his position. After carefully reading it, he asked many questions, and various views were exchanged. Finally Morris suggested that we visit Judge Kenny at his home in Hollywood. I called him up that evening and made an appointment to see him with Krishnaji the following week.

In the meantime I phoned Morris to get his personal reaction to Krishnaji's letter. "It looks to me as if he was had," he said, and added that the beginning and end of the letter had amused him.

"Why?" I asked.

"First he tells Rajagopal to drop dead, then at the end he signs off, 'With love.' Is that the custom in India?"

"No, it's Krishnaji's special style. But what makes you think love and death are incompatible?" This rejoinder led to a philosophical discussion totally unrelated to the case in question.

Some evenings later, Krishnaji, Mary Zimbalist, Alain Naude and I called on Robert Kenny at his home in Laurel Canyon. Kenny was acquainted with Krishnaji's teachings and was delighted to meet him. After he was filled in on the whole situation, he gave as his legal opinion that Krishnaji, or the Krishnamurti Foundation of America, had ample grounds to institute proceedings against Rajagopal and Krishnamurti Writings, Inc., but that it would take time before it came to a hearing, perhaps two years. Krishnaji was shocked to hear this. His highest priority, he said, was starting a school in Ojai to implement his teaching and his concept of education, but he could not go ahead because the funds and real estate which friends had given him through the years to propagate his teaching were presently tied up by Rajagopal and Krishnamurti Writings. Kenny responded by emphasizing the necessity of suing right away. He explained that the law gave a defendant the right to keep postponing a hearing on different grounds by filing demurrers, a tactic which could delay a legal resolution for years.

Krishnaji was impressed with Kenny's erudition and personal charm, and regretted that because of his position as a judge of the Superior Court he could not represent him. As it turned out, Mary Zimbalist's lawyers took over the case, which dragged on, through innumerable demurrers on the part of the defendant, for four years.

10

DURING THE YEARS OF LITIGATION I SAW KRISHNAJI OFTEN, sometimes once a week, at the Malibu home of Mary Zimbalist, where he spent several months of the year resting and preparing for his public lectures in Santa Monica and later in Ojai.

After telling me about Rajagopal's latest legal maneuver to postpone the hearing, and, again reiterating his wish to settle the whole thing amicably, he would walk with me along a narrow gravel path down the bluff to the beach.

There we would stroll along the surf as the ocean swallowed up the blazing sun, leaving the sky a mass of flaming color.

I was always amused at the way Krishnaji played like a child with the lapping waves, allowing a rolling wave nearly to spend itself and come within a few inches of his feet before jumping out of its way. I would try to imitate his little game, but not being as quick and light on my feet, I often failed to move fast enough and was thoroughly drenched. Once, however, Krishnaji himself was caught flat-footed by a particularly big wave when his attention was momentarily diverted by a dog—a friend of his, he said—who came bounding happily in greeting. Soaked from head to foot, he laughed heartily, and we continued our wave-dodging game until we were stopped, as always, by a forbidding chain-link fence. The fence emanated from one of the large beachfront homes and stretched across the full width of the beach into the water, forcing those who had the legal right to walk along an unobstructed beach to plunge into the ocean and swim around it to the other side. Krishnaji was always outraged at the sight of this arrogant impediment, erected in violation of the rights of ordinary citizens, and we wondered how much its rich and probably politically important owner had paid under the table to keep it there.

I never bothered him with personal problems on these informal beach walks. It was enough just to be with him, walking in silence, playing hopscotch with the waves, laughing over something trivial or making some casual remark about the spectacular sunset, taking in the little sandpipers scurrying along over the wet sand, the seagulls circling and wheeling and calling to each other, the sudden crash of a large swell striking a black rock, leaving it in a swirl of dripping white foam, a white sail in the distance. These were wonderful afternoons of quiet, simple delight, of wordless communion with each other and the environment. I could well understand how Robinson Jeffers would walk with him for an hour through the woods of Monterey Peninsula without saying a word.

My brother, John, died early in January, 1972. His death was totally unexpected and a great shock to me. John had been a photographer, a lover of adventure, women and wine, a man of great Latin charm. He had known Krishnaji as long as I had, and had many times delighted him with his stories and personal adventures. Krishnaji had just arrived from Europe and was staying in Malibu at the home of Mrs. Zimbalist. I called him to give him the sad news, saying I wanted to see him, and he asked me to come the following day for lunch.

He greeted me most affectionately. At the dining table I came right to the point: "Has John survived his bodily death in a subtler form? Yes or no?" There was a moment's silence. "My gut feeling," I went on, "is that he is here beside me, right now."

"Of course he is, right here beside you," said Krishnaji. "He's very close to you, and will continue being close for some time."

Two hours later we were still deep into the subject of death and the hereafter. He referred to that part of the personality that survives bodily death as an echo, instead of an astral body, as the Theosophists call it, the echo of the person who lived on earth, the duration of its life on the other side depending on the strength of the individual's earthly personality. "Dr. Besant's echo, for instance," he said, "will go on for a long time, for she had a very strong personality."

117

"Your viewpoint here is very similar to that of the Theosophists," I said.

"With one important difference," he replied. "There is no permanent substance that survives the death of the body. Whether the ego lasts one year, ten thousand, or a million years, it must finally come to an end."

Krishnaji's remarks during this conversation were among the most revealing and enlightening I had ever heard him make on the subject of death and survival beyond it. At the end of our talk Mrs. Zimbalist remarked that it was a great pity we had not recorded it, for, prodded by insistent questioning and probing on my part, and aided by a sympathetic Mrs. Zimbalist, Krishnaji had explored what to us was a new dimension on this fascinating subject.

Krishnaji has an extraordinary capacity for recall, when he wants to use that gift, and a few days later, he, Alain Naude and Mrs. Zimbalist recreated the entire conversation, this time recording it, with Naude asking Krishnaji essentially the same questions I had asked. It was staged in a much quieter atmosphere, naturally, and Naude's questions were cool and intellectual. They did not have the urgency and strong feeling of my approach, for I was hurting at the time. Nevertheless, I was fascinated when I heard the recording. It has not been published yet, but those few who heard it have remarked on its great impact. Krishnaji gave me permission to publish it in connection with this memoir, and it appears in the Appendix.

Some months later, Rajagopal and the board of directors of KWINC. sued Krishnamurti, the Krishnamurti Foundation of America and the foundation's trustees, claiming that they were interfering with Rajagopal's right to publish Krishnamurti's teachings as he saw fit. It was obvious that Rajagopal had no intention of settling the matter amicably.

The lawyers for the Krishnamurti Foundation pressed for an early hearing of their own suit, but Rajagopal, through his lawyers, kept asking for postponements, which baffled us all, as we had imagined, at the beginning of this unfortunate situation, that he would be most anxious to clear himself of the charges that had been made against him, and as early as possible.

During 1973–74 I saw Krishnaji on the average of two or three times a month while he stayed in Malibu. I usually arrived in the late afternoon, and we went for a long walk along the beach or up in the hills behind Mrs. Zimbalist's residence, in the neighborhood of the newly finished Pepperdine University, whose architecture of dirty-brown, barrack-like buildings Krishnaji did not admire. "They couldn't have made them uglier," he said on one of these walks as he stood contemplating them. "The triumph of mediocrity."

We stopped for a moment to watch the football squad in spring practice. He watched them with great interest for a moment, then turned to me and exclaimed, "Educated morons!" He went on to comment sadly on the enormous amounts of money spent yearly to turn out these mediocrities.

We talked about India. The previous year friends both in the United States and in India, aware that he always spoke his mind regardless of consequences, had warned him not to visit India because of its increasingly repressive rule regarding dissenters and anyone daring to criticize Indira Gandhi's policies. Krishnaji went anyway in 1976, after being assured by Mrs. Gandhi, who was a personal friend of many years' standing, that he would not be interfered with regardless of what he said. Later Mrs. Gandhi made the startling announcement that there would be free elections throughout the country. I asked Krishnaji what had brought about such a sudden change in her dictatorial rule. "The masses continue starving while the few get richer," he answered. "There's corruption at every level of government. India is in bad shape."

"Did you see Mrs. Gandhi this time?"

"Yes, I had a long talk with her."

"Did your talk have anything to do with the decision to have free elections?"

Krishnaji thought for a long moment, a half smile on his face. Then he said, "Maybe."*

Krishnaji was always amused by the way people all over the world were continually taken by their so-called leaders: the blind leading the blind. I couldn't entirely agree with him. Certainly some persons were much more dangerous than others, I argued, reflecting that it was essential to try to create an atmosphere in society so that intelligence would have some chance of functioning, regardless of whether people were free in his sense of the word. He agreed with me on this point, saying that while the really important thing was to free yourself from all conditioning, you don't stand back and do nothing just because you are not inwardly free.

He then asked me if I was still on the staff of the Southern California Counseling Center. He knew its founder, Dr. Ben Weininger, and referred people to him "if

---

* Pupul Jayakar, in her 1986 biography of Krishnamurti, is a great deal more explicit. It was she who had first brought Mrs. Gandhi together with K, in the 1950s; she had also invited both of them to a dinner party in October 1976 during the state of emergency. At that dinner the prime minister requested a private interview, after which "she came out of the room visibly moved, and tears were streaming down her face . . . In later years she told me that it was on October 28, 1976, the day she met Krishnaji for the second time, a frail movement had awakened in her, suggesting an end to emergency, whatever the consequences" (pp. 342–343).

they had neurotic problems." Krishnaji and I had often discussed the value of psychotherapy, which he generally minimized, admitting that just talking to someone about one's problems often did help.

"Yes, I'm still at the center officially," I told him, "but I'm now working where the heat really is, with a bunch of angry, rebellious kids at Juvenile Hall."

"Do you counsel them?" he asked.

"I mostly listen to them. They've been counseled and talked to all their lives, but seldom has anyone ever really listened to them."

Krishnaji did not deny the value of this kind of therapy, but only as a temporary help. He talked of a radical transformation of the individual as the only true and lasting psychotherapy and reminded me of a story he had told me years before, about a man he had healed of a physical illness, but who later ended up in jail.

We were walking briskly downhill on the way back home when Krishnaji abruptly stopped in the middle of the street, bent over and picked up something underfoot. He held it gently in the palm of his hand and showed it to me. It was a ladybug. Then he proceeded to give it a serious lecture on the dangers of lying on a street where trucks travel up and down. He took it across the street and deposited it safely near some wild flowers. Passing by the neatly kept gridiron of Pepperdine University, Krishnaji cast a quick glance in its direction and said, "Education is the key to it . . . but not that kind." Then he talked about the school he had founded many years ago in the Rishi Valley of northern India, the school at Brockwood Park in England, the new school he wanted to build in Ojai. This subject filled him with enthusiasm. He saw in education the key to a real transformation of society.

121

I knew Krishnaji had unusual healing power, although he disliked talking about it, and when we got home I asked him if he could help my eyes, which were badly irritated, mostly, I think, because of the heavy smog which often covers Los Angeles. He immediately acceded to my request and asked me to sit on a hard chair. Standing behind me, he placed his hands over my eyes for a minute or so. Then he slowly drew them up over my forehead and head, repeating this procedure for ten or fifteen minutes. Afterward my eyes felt wonderfully clear and refreshed, and I had a delightful sense of well-being and inner peace. Krishnaji was most generous with these magnetic, healing treatments while at Malibu, and I figured that my eyes would never trouble me again. But during his long stay away from the country, the smog and the stress and strain of city living, plus long hours of writing at night, would affect them again, until his welcome return.

Toward the end of 1973 my sister Flora died. Krishnaji had known her well; she had been a great admirer of his. I wrote him about her death, and he quickly answered, remembering to inquire about my eyes.

2nd January 1974.

My dear Sidney,
Thank you very much for your letter of November the 6th.

I am so sorry about your sister, and you do seem to be having a difficult time and I hope you are well and not too heavily burdened with all the recent deaths.

I had been to different parts of India—Delhi in the north, Madras in the south, Bangalore also in the south and then Bombay and from there I will be leaving at the end of the month, a few days in Rome, a couple of more days in Brockwood Park and I hope to be in California on the 5th of February. So, I hope there will be an opportunity for us to meet.

I wonder how your eyes are and I hope you are well and are looking after yourself.

With much affection,

J.K.

In February Krishnaji was back in Malibu at Mrs. Zimbalist's. I telephoned to say hello and they invited me over for lunch. This was an occasion I especially remember, because for the first time, thirty-six years after that marvelously joyous and deeply stirring experience I had known while listening to his opening talk at Castle Eerde, I talked to him at length about the whole thing: the great "high" it gave me at the time, the period that followed when I lost it, then my rediscovery of it months later while meditating in the Hollywood Hills, followed by its eventual loss once again in the hustle and bustle of daily living and the pressures of handling the complicated family business affairs while writing to earn a living.

He listened most attentively, occasionally breaking into the narrative with a short remark: "You were too anxious about it. You should have just let it happen." When I was through, there was a moment's silence. Then he said: "What a great pity. You probably were close to a breakthrough. What a great pity."

At any rate, I was very happy to have spoken to him at last about that inner explosion he had triggered in me so many years before, which had been so meaningful in my life.

After lunch we walked leisurely over to my car, parked near the garage, where he showed me Mrs. Zimbalist's new Mercedes Benz. It was a beautiful, bottle-green two-door sedan which had just arrived from Europe. He said he wanted to give it a good polishing, and as he had always admired the clean, polished look on my old Buick Riviera, he asked me if I would get him some of the same polish I had been using on mine. A week later I returned with a can of polishing wax. He had just washed the Mercedes and was waiting for me. Immediately we set upon the new car, exchanging the can of wax back and forth as each of us tackled one side of the car. Krishnaji was meticulously careful about applying the stuff. Examining my side of the car, he caught a couple of very small spots on the rear fender where the wax had not been evenly applied, and called my attention to them. Then came the strenuous job of polishing, which Krishnaji attacked with professional zeal. The car shone like a newly cut emerald. Mrs. Zimbalist came over to ask us to come in for a cup of tea, and stood admiring our handiwork. She assured us we could count on her recommendation as a good team of car polishers.

The car was driven into the garage and the door tightly closed. When I inquired about the reason for taking such precautions in plain daylight, Krishnaji replied, "To keep the rats out." Then he explained that a few days earlier, when they had taken the car to the agency, a mechanic had found a big rat cozily ensconced in the undercarriage, near the radiator. The discriminating rodent had gathered some old rags and made its nest there, and had apparently been happily riding with Krishnaji for days in great style.

Krishnaji's increasing concern with the importance of education and the establishment of a Krishnamurti school and center in Ojai dominated his activities at this time. There were many meetings and discussions, with Krishnaji often becoming impatient when reminded of the enormous cost of such an undertaking. "You people of little faith!" he once exclaimed at a meeting, stressing again the urgency of rechanneling education.

Large funds were needed, and everyone tried to help. My very small contribution consisted of bringing a wealthy gentleman friend of mine, who knew about the school plans and the need for money, over to Mrs. Zimbalist's to meet Krishnaji. Mrs. Zimbalist was a charming hostess, and the occasion turned out to be a pleasant social afternoon. But the gentleman in question was much more interested in pushing his own pet project, than in furthering Krishnaji's. He proposed having a seminar at Saanen attended by prominent leaders in education, psychiatry, and the arts, a group he had collected around himself, to share the platform with Krishnaji in discussing world problems. Krishnaji's answer was short and to the point. "At Saanen," he said, "only this dog barks." The potential contributor took a last gulp of tea and the conversation became noticeably chilly. So ended my fund-raising efforts.

I saw Krishnaji that spring at other times before his series of talks at Libby Park in Ojai. He was in great physical shape for a man in his late seventies and appeared to be enjoying life hugely. Whenever I asked him how the Rajagopal affair was getting along, he would tell me about the latest postponement, and there would be just a shadow of sadness in his eyes. "They must be mad, those people," he would say.

Late of an April afternoon we went for a walk along the Malibu beach, a cool sea breeze blowing in our faces. Krishnaji was more talkative this time than on previous strolls. The beach was unusually deserted; even the sea gulls were scarce. The great empty space and the calm, blue sea were exhilarating. "I suppose if one could see clairvoyantly out there the place wouldn't appear so empty," I said. "People, sea elementals . . ."

He interrupted. "The place is full of them. I pay no attention to them."

"Do you see them every time you come out here?"

"Only when I want to."

Since the subject had been broached, I took this opportunity to ask him about Invisible Helpers. "Do such people really exist?"

"Why not?" he said. "Any decent person in this world will help another when in need. Why not on the other side? What's so special about it?"

Since he was in a talkative mood, I thought I'd take advantage of it and asked him point-blank what he thought his life would have been like if Dr. Besant and C. W. Leadbeater had not taken care of him in his early years and sponsored him. He was thoughtfully silent for a long moment. Then he said, "I probably would have died of malnutrition."

"Do you think you would have been a liberated man, whatever that means, without the background they provided?"

A much quicker answer: "Yes. It might have taken longer, but the end result would have been the same. I probably would have become a *sanyasi*.* The drive was there. Nothing could have finally thwarted it." Then he said something that surprised me because it sounded out of character: "One of India's best known astrologers cast my horoscope when I was very young, and said I would become a *Jivanmukta* (liberated man)." He laughed lightheartedly, as if to stress the unimportance of such weighty predictions.

---

* A Hindu holy man who lives a life of complete renunciation.

I wanted to continue this unusual dialogue, but one of those deceptive waves that suddenly rise out of nowhere was upon us. Although we jumped to get out of its way, it splashed us from head to foot. Krishnaji laughed with fun, a laughter I always enjoyed hearing for its quality of pure delight. The moment for serious talk was over. The beach stroll had ended. We were heading home atop the bluff.

On December 26, 1974, Superior Court Judge Richard Heaton announced that an out-of-court settlement had been reached between the Krishnamurti Foundation and Rajagopal's newly named Krishnamurti and Rajagopal Foundation. Both parties agreed that no one would elaborate on the settlement beyond what was contained in the release and approved by Judge Heaton.

It soon became apparent, however, that Arya Vihara was one of the properties that had been transferred to the Krishnamurti Foundation, for Krishnaji, who had returned from India earlier than usual, was making plans to go back to his former Ojai home. Also, it was evident that the Oak Grove property had been awarded to the Krishnamurti Foundation as well, for it was announced that the spring talks in 1975 were to be held in the grove.

The long, drawn-out controversy had finally been settled. But by official edict the lips of the litigants had been sealed as to the provisions of the settlement. On December 27, the *Ventura County Star-Free Press* published an article detailing some of the terms:

KRISHNAMURTI SETTLEMENT REACHED

A lengthy court battle between the Indian philosopher Jiddu Krishnamurti and some of his erstwhile followers over title to his writings, and to property, has ended in Ventura Superior Court.

. . . Superior Court Judge Richard C. Heaton approved

the settlement in a brief hearing Thursday. A press release, agreed to by the parties, was issued, with a stipulation, approved by the court, that neither would make any further statement.

As part of the settlement, both Krishnamurti and directors of Krishnamurti Writings Inc. (KWINC) agreed to withdraw allegations made against each other, and to dismiss all legal claims.

Also, KWINC is to be dissolved, its assets and functions being divided between Krishnamurti Foundation of America (the organization the philosopher founded as a proposed successor to KWINC) and K & R Foundation. The latter was set up by J. Rajagopal of Ojai and others.

The stipulation also provides that "all previous writing, understandings or agreements" between the parties are superseded.

Krishnaji's long exile from his Ojai home, Arya Vihara, was over. After the announcement we stood on the high cliff in Mrs. Zimbalist's garden overlooking the late afternoon sea and talked about the unnecessary effort and money that had to be spent to arrive at a settlement that could have been reached years before quietly and amicably. A shadow of sadness crossed his dark, luminous eyes. Then suddenly they were full of light and humor as a hare darted out in front of him, headed for a small vegetable garden nearby, where appetizing green things were growing. He told me he had been trying to keep the persistent little creature away from it, had in fact been keeping his eye on it in the afternoon when the soft-treading rascal sneaked in to have his garden-fresh salad. But evidently the alert cottontail had also been keeping its eye on Krishnaji, for it made a neat end run around him as he talked to me and dashed straight for the succulent lettuce. It was a daring maneuver. We watched it in admiration and laughed. Soon the furry little thief was out of sight, and probably out of reach, so we left him there to his vegetarian diet. It had that in common with us.

On the way back to my car I said I was so happy he was returning to Arya Vihara, but also there was a bit of sadness in it for me. He turned and looked surprised. "I won't be seeing you as often, Krishnaji. Ojai is so much further away from Hollywood than Malibu."

"You can always see me any time you want to," he replied.

We were close to the main entrance. He excused himself and went indoors, asking me to wait. When he returned a moment later, he presented me with a handsome beret he had worn in Europe. "Will it fit? It hasn't been worn much," he said apologetically.

It fit perfectly. I gave him a tight Costa Rican *abrazo* (hug).

As we stood by the car, he looked away at the rolling hills beyond the highway, with their new spring carpet of deep yellow wild mustard, swaying gently in the breeze. "Such beauty!" he exclaimed. "Such beauty!" He was totally absorbed in the scene before him. I gazed at him and envied him. How wonderful to be thrilled to the marrow and swept away by the simple sight of a mustard-covered hillside!

As I was leaving, Krishnaji asked me a question he had asked before several times—whether I had finally tackled the memoir of our long friendship which I had promised to write.

"I've started it," I said hesitantly, conscious that I had done only a short outline and that I kept postponing the real writing.

"You're lazy. Get to work on it," he said firmly.

After I got home, I took out the brief outline and started seriously putting it all together.

Mrs. Zimbalist eventually sold her Malibu home and built an equally handsome residence in Ojai, next to Krishnaji's cottage, connecting both of them. With that childlike enthusiasm and bubbling interest that was so typical of him, he showed me his renovated cottage that I had known so well in the old days, pointing delightedly at all the modern improvements. It had been beautifully redecorated, but it still had the same characteristics as of old, a simplicity that verged on the austere, a sun-filled airiness and a sense of peace and repose. He spent several months of the year there, resting from his strenuous European and Indian lecture schedules and preparing for his spring talks and discussions in the Oak Grove.

Krishnamurti, a spiritual genius without peer in the world, had been "singing his song" for over fifty years, emphasizing now a certain note, now another one, and now still another. Hundreds of thousands of people throughout the world have listened to him, and whether his words have brought new insights and vision, or none; confusion and disappointment or clarity and purpose; whatever the individual response, there is no question that his main theme remained steady and clear throughout: to free the individual from the crushing burden of his environment, his conditioned thought, his inherited fears, his crippling prejudices.

He said: "You are accustomed to listening to the song of another, and so your hearts are empty, and they will always be empty because you fill your hearts with the song of another. That is not your song; then you are merely gramophones, changing the records according to the moods, but you are not musicians. And especially in times of great travail and trouble we have to be musicians, each one of us; we have to recreate ourselves with song, which means to free and to empty the heart of those things which are filled by the mind. Therefore, we have to understand the creations of the mind, and see the falseness of those creations. Then, when the heart is empty—not, as in your case, filled with ashes—when the heart is empty and the mind is quiet, then there is a song, the song that cannot be destroyed or perverted because it is not put together by the mind."

Many of us have listened to him for a lifetime. We discussed our problems with him, unburdened our innermost selves to him; we have been inspired and renewed, have shed many fears and prejudices, have attained some maturity. Some of us have probably had glimpses of that extra dimension Krishnamurti has called the Unknown. But I think it safe to say that none of us has caught the fire that burned in him. We are not singing our own songs.

Why is that? Is Krishnamurti one of a kind? Other great spiritual teachers in the past appear to have been so: Buddha, Christ, Lao-tzu. Krishnamurti would probably reject this idea as simply an excuse, a justification for not tackling ourselves with complete attention. Perhaps it is. Nevertheless, I once asked him why there appeared to be no other Krishnamurtis in the world, even though he had been talking for half a century. He answered: "A tree needs space around it if it is to grow into a great tree. It cannot attain its full growth if it is too close to another great tree."

Perhaps we have been crowding the great teacher, psychologically speaking, in our too-eager attempt to cross over into the realm of non-ego he referred to as the Ultimate Good. Perhaps, to paraphrase his own words, because our mind-heart does not sing, we have instead pursued the Singer, thus missing the essential meaning of the Song.

Will Krishnamurti's spiritual legacy to the world be

another Krishnamurti in the future to give voice again to the Passionate Song? More realistically, it is likely to be a slow and gradual transformation of the psyche in a few people, here and there, to a passive, non-judgmental, sensitively aware state of mind that perceives things as they are, an inner quality of the spirit I would venture to call "ardent listlessness," a term the poet John Keats used with great insight in a stanza of his long poem "Endymion":

And truly I would rather be struck dumb
Than speak against this ardent listlessness:
For I have thought that it might bless
The world with benefits unknowingly;
As does the nightingale, up-perched high,
And cloistered among cool and bunched leaves.

Epilogue

KRISHNAMURTI DIED ON THE NIGHT OF FEBRUARY 16, 1986, after a brief bout with cancer. He had come back a few weeks before from India to die at Pine Cottage on the Arya Vihara estate in his beloved Ojai Valley. It was here, under a pepper tree, that he had begun his sometimes painful spiritual journey in 1922.

During his final days many people who had known and loved Krishnamurti gathered from all over the world. One of them was the scientist Asit Chandmal, a trustee of the Indian Krishnamurti Foundation and author of a book celebrating K's eighty-fifth birthday. As Chandmal sat with him at Pine Cottage, Krishnamurti, who had known him since he was two years old, asked:

"What are you anchored in, sir?"

After a moment's hesitation, Asit Chandmal answered: "In you, sir."

"I'm gone," Krishnamurti replied.

Sidney Field was planning to visit his sick friend in Ojai on February 17. He telephoned Arya Vihara to ask when would be the best time to come, and that is how he found out that Krishnaji had died. A little over two years later, having been unusually strong and young for his years, Sidney himself became sick. A lifelong vegetarian, he stopped eating altogether. The doctors suspected cancer, but he refused to stay in the hospital, even for the tests. During those last days, Eve Tettemer Siegel, whom he had known and loved all his life, visited him several times in his Hollywood house. They often talked about Krishnaji, and Sidney would tell stories of the good times they had.

The last time Eve went to see him, Sidney was very weak. He was sitting in a chair and seemed to be going in and out of sleep. To bring him back and to take his mind off his physical condition, Eve asked him, "Do you see Krishnaji?"

Sidney smiled, his face suddenly free of pain.

"Not yet, sweetheart, not yet."

A few days later, on July 21, 1988, he did.

Appendix

A CONVERSATION FOLLOWING THE DEATH
OF JOHN FIELD
PARTICIPANTS: KRISHNAMURTI,
ALAIN NAUDE,
MARY ZIMBALIST
RECORDED ON JANUARY 14, 1972

KRISHNAMURTI: We said the other day Sidney Field came to see me. His brother John died recently. You knew him. He was very concerned whether his brother was living in a different level of consciousness; whether there was John as an entity born [in the] next

135

life. And did I believe in reincarnation, and what did it mean. And so he had lots of questions. He was having a difficult time with himself because of his brother, whom he loved and whom we have known for years and years. So out of that conversation two things came up. First, is there a permanent ego? If there is such a thing as a permanent something, then what is its relationship from the present to the future? The future being next life or ten years later. But if you admit or accept or believe or assert that there is a permanent ego, then reincarnation . . .

ALAIN NAUDE: . . . is inevitable.

K: Not inevitable. I wouldn't say inevitable. It is plausible, because the permanent ego, to me, if it is permanent, can be changed in ten years' time. It can incarnate differently in ten years' time.

A: We read this all the time in the Indian scriptures. We read about children who remember the past life, about a little girl who said, "What am I doing here? My home is in some other village. I'm married to so and so. I have three children." And in many cases I believe that this has been verified.

K: I don't know. So there is that. If there is no permanent entity, then what is reincarnation? Both involve time, both involve a movement in space. Space being environment, relationship, pressure, all that existing within that space, time.

A: Within time and temporal circumstances . . .

K: . . . That is, culture, etcetera . . .

A: . . . Within some sort of social set-up.

K: So is there a permanent me? Obviously not. But Sidney said, "Then what is it that I feel, that John is with me? When I enter the room, I know he is there. I'm not fooling myself, I'm not imagining; I feel him there as I feel my sister who was in that room yesterday. It's as clear, as definite as that."

A: And also, sir, when you say "obviously not," would you explain that?

K: But wait. So he says, "My brother is there." I said of course he is there, because first of all you have your association and memories of John and that is projected, and that projection is your remembrance.

A: So that the John who was contained within you is that.

K: And when John lived he was associated with you. His presence is with you. When he was living, you might not have seen him all day, but his presence was in that room.

A: His presence was there, and perhaps this is what people mean when they speak of an aura.

K: No, aura is different. Let's not push that in yet.

MARY ZIMBALIST: May I interrupt—when you say he was in that room, whether alive or dead, was there something external to his brother and his sister that was there, or was it in their consciousness?

K: It is both in their consciousness and outside consciousness. I can project my brother and say he was with me last night, feeling he was with me, that may emanate from me; or John, who died ten days ago—his atmosphere, his thoughts, his way of behaving still remaining there, even though physically he might have gone.

A: The psychic momentum.

K: The physical heat.

Z: Are you saying there is a sort of energy, for want of a different word, which human beings give off?

K: There was a photograph of a parking lot taken where there had been many cars, and the photo showed, although there were no cars there, the form of the cars that had been there.

A: Yes. I saw that.

K: That is, the heat that the car had left came on the negative.

A: And also one day when we were all living in Gstaad, the first time I was your guest at Gstaad, we were living at Les Capris— you left for America before any of us left, and I went into that flat—you were still alive and on your way to America and your presence was there, extremely strong.

K: That's it.

A: Your presence was so strong, one felt one could touch you. This was not simply because I was thinking about you before I entered the flat.

K: So there are three possibilities. I project out of my remembrance and consciousness, or pick up the residual energy of John.

A: Like a smell which would linger.

K: John's thought or John's existence is still there.

A: That's the third possibility.

Z: What do you mean by that, John's existence?

A: That John is really there as before he died? The third possibility.

K: I live in a room for a number of years. The presence of that room contained my energy, my thoughts, my feelings.

A: It contains its own energy, and when we go into a new house it sometimes takes time before you are rid of the person who was there before you, even though you may not have known him.

K: So those are the three possibilities. And the other is John's thought, because John clings to life. John's desires are there in the air, not in the room.

A: Immaterially.

K: Yes, they are there just like a thought.

A: And does that mean that John is conscious and there is a being who is self-conscious calling himself John, thinking those thoughts?

K: I doubt it.

A: I think that is what the people who believe in reincarnation would postulate.

K: See what happens, sir. This makes four possibilities and the idea that John whose physical body is gone, exists in thought.

A: In his own thought or someone else's?

K: In his own thought.

A: Exists as a thinking entity?

K: As a thinking entity exists.

A: As a conscious being.

K: That is—listen to this, it's rather interesting—John continues because he is the world of vulgarity, of greed, of envy, of drinking, and of competition. That is the common pattern of man. It continues and John may be identified with that, or is that.

A: John is the desires, the thoughts, the beliefs, the associations.

K: Of the world.

A: Which are incarnate and which are material.

K: Which is the world—which is everybody.

A: This is a big thing you are saying. It would be nice if you could explain it a little better. When you say John persists, John continues because there is the continuation of the vulgar in him—the vulgar being worldly, material association.

K: That's right: fear, wanting power, position.

A: Desire to be as an entity.

K: So that, because that is a common thing of the world, he is of the world and the world does incarnate.

A: You say the world does incarnate.

K: Take the mass of the people. They are caught in this stream and that stream goes on. I may have a son who is part of that stream and in that stream there is John also, as a human being who is caught in it. And my son may remember some of John's attitudes.

A: Ah, but you are saying something different.

K: Yes.

A: You are saying that John is contained in all the memories that different people have of him. In that respect we can see that he does exist. Because I remember a friend of mine died not long ago, and it was very clear to me when I thought about it that in fact he was very much alive in the memories of all the people who had loved him.

K: That's just it.

A: Therefore, he was not absent from the world, he was still in the stream of events which we call the world, which is the lives of different people who had associated with him. In that sense we see that he can perhaps live forever.

K: Unless he breaks away from it—breaks away from the stream. A man who is not vulgar—let's use that word, vulgar, representing all this . . . greed, envy, power, position, hatred, desires, all that—let's call that vulgar. Unless I am free from the vulgar, I will continue representing the whole of vulgarity, the whole vulgarity of man.

A: Yes, I will be that vulgarity by pursuing it, and in fact incarnating in it, giving it life.

K: Therefore I incarnate in that vulgarity. That is, first I can project John, my brother.

A: In my thought and imagination or remember him. The second point, I can pick up his kinetic energy, which is still around.

K: His smell, his taste, his saying the words.

A: The pipe which is unsmoked on the desk, the half-finished letter.

K: All that.

A: Flowers he picked in the garden.

K: Third, the thought remains in the room.

A: Thought remains in the room?

K: Feelings . . .

A: One might say, the psychic equivalent of his kinetic energy.

K: Yes.

A: His thought remains almost as a material smell. As a physical smell.

K: That's right.

A: The energy of thought remains like an old coat that you hang up.

K: Thought, will, if he has a very strong will; active desires and thought, they also remain.

A: But that's not different from the third point. The third point is that thought remains, which is will, which is desire.

K: The fourth point in the stream of vulgarity.

A: That's not very clear.

K: Look, sir, I live an ordinary life, like millions and millions of people.

A: Yes, pursuing goals, hopes and fears.

K: I live the usual life. A little more refined, a little bit higher or lower, along the same current, I follow that current. I am that current. Me, who is that current, is bound to continue in that stream, which is the stream of me. I'm not different from millions of other people.

A: Therefore are you saying, sir, even dead I continue because the things which were me are continuing.

K: In the human being.

A: Therefore, I survive. I was not different from the things which filled and preoccupied my life.

K: That's right.

A: Since these things which filled and occupied my life survive, in a manner of speaking I survive since they do.

K: That's right. That's four points.

A: The question is about the fifth. Is there a conscious thinking entity who knows that he is conscious when everybody has said, "There goes poor old John," even put him in the ground. Is there a conscious entity who immaterially says, "Good gracious, they've put that body in the ground but I have consciousness of being alive."

K: Yes.

A: That is the question which I think is difficult to answer.

K: Sidney was asking that question.

A: Because we see that everybody does exist in these other ways after death.

K: Now, you are asking the question, Does John, whose body is burned—cremated—does that entity continue to live?

A: Does that entity continue to have its consciousness of its own existence?

145

K: I question whether there is a separate John.

A: You said at the beginning, is there such a thing as a permanent ego? You said obviously not.

K: When you say that John, my brother, is dead and ask whether he is living, living in a separate consciousness, I question whether he was ever separate from the stream.

A: Yes.

K: You follow what I am saying, sir?

A: Was there a John alive?

K: When John was alive, was he different from the stream?

A: The stream filled his consciousness of himself. His consciousness of himself was the stream knowing itself.

K: No, sir, just go slowly. It's rather complicated. The stream of humanity is anger, hate, jealousy, seeking power, position, cheating, corrupt, polluted. That is the stream. Of that stream is my brother John. When he existed physically, he had a physical body, but psychologically he was of this. Therefore was he ever different from this? From the stream? Or only physically different and therefore thinking he was different. You follow my point?

A: There was an entity who was self-conscious . . .

K: . . . As John.

A: He was self-conscious, and the stream was in relationship to himself.

K: Yes.

A: My wife, my child, my love.

K: But was John inwardly different from the stream? That's my point. Therefore what is dead is the body. And the continuation of John is part of that stream. I, as his brother, would like to think of him as separate because he lived with me as a separate being physically. Inwardly he was of the stream. Therefore, was there a John who was different from the stream? And, if he was different, then what happens? I don't know if you follow.

A: There is a stream from outside and there is a stream from inside. Vulgarity seen in the street is different from the man who feels himself to be acting in the moment of that vulgarity. I insult somebody. This is vulgarity. You see that vulgarity from outside and you say there is a vulgar act. I who am insulting somebody see the act in a different way. I feel self-conscious life at the moment when I insult. In fact I insult because there is a conscious thinking about me. I am protecting myself, so I insult.

147

K: My point is, this is what is happening with one hundred million people. Millions of people. As long as I swim in that stream, am I different? Is the real John different from the stream?

A: Was there ever a John?

K: That's all my point.

A: There was conscious determination which felt itself to be John.

K: Yes, but I can imagine. I can invent because I'm different.

A: There was imagination, thought, calling itself John.

K: Yes, sir.

A: Now, does that thought still call itself John?

K: But I belong to that stream.

A: You always belong to the stream.

K: There is no separate entity as John who was my brother, who is now dead.

A: Are you saying that there was no individual?

K: No, this is what we call permanent. The permanent ego is this.

Z: What we think is individual.

K: Individual, the collective, the self.

A: Yes, the creation of thought which calls itself self.

K: It is of this stream.

A: That's right.

K: Therefore, was there ever a John? There is only a John when he is out of the stream.

A: That's right.

K: So first we are trying to find out if there is a permanent ego which incarnates.

A: The nature of the ego is impermanent.

K: Reincarnation is in the whole of Asia, and the modern people who believe in it say there is a permanent ego. You take many lives so that it can become dissolved and be absorbed in Brahma and all that. Now, is there from the beginning a permanent entity, an entity that lasts centuries and centuries? There is no such permanent entity, obviously. I like to think I'm permanent. My permanence is identified with my furniture, my wife, my husband, circumstances. These are words and images of thought. I don't actually possess that chair. I call it mine.

A: Exactly. You think it's a chair and you own it.

K: I like to think I own it.

A: But it's just an idea.

149

K: So, watch it. So there is no permanent self.
       If there was a permanent self, it would be
       this stream. Now, realizing that I am like
       the rest of the world, that there is no sepa-
       rate K, or John, as my brother, then I can
       incarnate if I step out of it. Incarnate in
       the sense that the change can take place
       away from the stream. In the stream there
       is no change.

A: If there is permanence, it is outside of the
       stream.

K: No, sir, permanency, semipermanency, is
       the stream.

A: And therefore it is not permanent. If it is
       permanent, it is not the stream. Therefore,
       if there is an entity, then it must be out of
       the stream. Therefore, that which is true,
       that which is permanent, is not a some-
       thing.

K: It is not in the stream.

A: That's right.

K: When Naude dies, as long as he belongs to
       the stream, that stream and its flow is
       semipermanent.

A: Yes. It goes on. It's a historical thing.

K: But if Naude says, I will incarnate, not in
       the next life, now, tomorrow, which
       means I will step out of the stream, he is

no longer belonging to the stream; therefore there is nothing permanent.

A: There is nothing to reincarnate. Therefore, that which reincarnates, if reincarnation is possible, is not permanent anyway.

K: No, it's the stream.

A: It's very temporal.

K: Don't put it that way.

A: A separate entity is not real.

K: No, as long as I belong to the stream . . .

A: I don't really exist . . .

K: There is no separate entity. I am the world.

A: That's right.

K: When I step out of the world, is there a me to continue?

A: Exactly. It's beautiful.

K: So, what we are trying to do is to justify the existence of the stream.

A: Is that what we are trying to do?

K: Of course, when I say I must have many lives and therefore I must go through the stream.

A: What we are trying to do, then, is we are trying to establish that we are different from the stream.

K: We are not.

A: We are not different from the stream.

K: So, sir, then what happens? If there is no permanent John or K or Naude or Zimbalist, what happens? You remember, sir, I think I read it in the Tibetan tradition or some other tradition, that when a person dies, is dying, the priest or the monk comes in and sends all the family away, locks the door and says to the dying man, "Look you're dying—let go—let all of your antagonisms, all your worldliness, all your ambition, let go, because you are going to meet a light in which you will be absorbed, if you let go. If not, you'll come back. Which is, come back to the stream. You will be the stream again.

A: Yes.

K: So what happens to you if you step out of the stream?

A: You step out of the stream, you cease to be, but the you which was, was only created by thought, anyway.

K: Which is the stream.

A: Vulgarity.

K: Vulgarity. What happens if you step out of the stream? The stepping out is the incarnation. Yes, sir, but that is a new thing you are coming into. There is a new dimension coming into being.

A: Yes.

K: Now, what happens? You follow? Naude has stepped out of the stream. What happens? You are not an artist. Not a businessman. You are not a politician, not a musician, all that identification is part of the stream.

A: All the qualities.

K: All the qualities. When you discard all that, what happens?

A: You have no identity.

K: Identity is here. Say, for instance, Napoleon, or any of these so-called world leaders: they killed, they butchered, they did every horror imaginable, they lived and died in the stream, they were of the stream. That is very simple and very clear. There is a man who steps out of the stream.

A: Before physical death?

K: Of course; otherwise there is no point.

A: Therefore, another dimension is born.

K: What happens?

A: The ending of the dimension which is familiar to us is another dimension, but it cannot be postulated at all because all postulation is in terms of the dimension we are in.

K: Yes, but suppose you, living now . . .

A: Step out of it.

K: Step out of the stream. What happens?

A: This is death, sir.

K: No, sir.

A: This is death, but not physical death.

K: You see, you step out of it. What happens?

A: Nothing can be said about what happens.

K: Wait, sir. You see, none of us step out of the river, and we are always from the river, trying to reach the other shore.

A: It's like people talking about deep sleep from awakeness.

K: That's it, sir. We belong to this stream, all of us. Man does belong to the stream and from the stream he wants to reach that shore, never leaving the river. Now the man says, all right, I see the fallacy of this, the absurdity of my position.

A: You can't state another dimension from the old dimension.

K: So I leave that. So the mind says, "Out!" He steps out and what takes place? Don't verbalize it.

A: The only thing that one can say about it in terms of the stream is silence. Because it is the silence of the stream, and one can also say it is the death of the stream. Therefore, in terms of the stream it is sometimes called oblivion.

K: You know what it means to step out of the stream: no character.

A: No memory.

K: No, sir, see: no character, because the moment you have character it's of the stream. The moment you say you are virtuous, you are of the stream—or not virtuous. To step out of the stream is to step out of this whole structure. So, creation as we know it is in the stream. Mozart, Beethoven, you follow, the painters, they are all here.

A: I think perhaps, sir, sometimes that which is in the stream is vivified, as it were, from something which is beyond.

K: No, no, can't be. Don't say these things because I can create in the stream. I can paint marvelous pictures. Why not? I can compose the most extraordinary symphonies, all the technique . . .

A: Why are they extraordinary?

K: Because the world needs it. There is the need, the demand, and the supply. I'm saying to myself what happens to the man who really steps out. Here in the river, in the stream, energy is in conflict, in contradiction, in strife, in vulgarity. But that's going on all the time . . .

A: Me and you.

K: Yes, that's going on all the time. When he steps out of it, there is no conflict, there is no division as my country, your country.

A: No division.

K: No division. So what is the quality of that man, that mind that has no sense of division? It is pure energy, isn't it? So our concern is this stream and stepping out of it.

A: That is meditation, that is real meditation, because the stream is not life. The stream is totally mechanical.

K: I must die to the stream.

A: All the time.

K: All the time. And therefore I must deny—not deny, I must not get entangled with—John who is in the stream.

A: One must repudiate the things of the stream.

K: That means I must repudiate my brother.

A: I must repudiate having a brother. You see what it means?

K: I see my brother belonging to this, and as I move away from the stream my mind is open. I think that is compassion.

A: When the stream is seen from that which is not of the stream.

K: When the man of the stream steps out and looks, then he has compassion.

A: And love.

K: So, you see, sir, reincarnation, that is, incarnating over and over again, is in the stream. This is not a very comforting thing. I come to you and tell you my brother died yesterday, and you tell me this. I call you a terribly cruel man. But you are weeping for yourself, you are weeping for me, for the stream. That's why people don't want to know. I want to know where my brother is, not whether he is.

SELECTED READING

Asit Chandmal: *A Thousand Moons—Krishnamurti at Eighty-five.* New York. Harry N. Abrams, 1985.

Lilly Heber. *Krishnamurti—The Man and His Message.* London: George Allen and Unwin, 1931.

Pupul Jayakar. *Krishnamurti—A Biography.* New York: Harper & Row, 1986.

Mary Lutyens. *Krishnamurti—The Years of Awakening.* London: John Murray, 1975.

————. *Krishnamurti—The Years of Fulfilment.* London: John Murray, 1983.

————. *Krishnamurti—The Open Door.* London: John Murray, 1988.

Gertrude M. Williams. *The Passionate Pilgrim—A Life of Annie Besant.* London: John Hamilton Ltd., n.d.